SELF PUBLISHING

IN THE

DIGITAL AGE

AN AUTHOR'S GUIDE

PUBLISHING FOR

PRINT ON DEMAND AND E-BOOKS

BY

STEVEN HODDER

TAKAHE PUBLISHING LTD.

2014

This edition published 2014 by:
Takahe Publishing Ltd.
Registered Office:
77 Earlsdon Street, Coventry CV5 6EL

Copyright ©Takahe Publishing Ltd. 2014
ISBN 978-1-908837-01-1

***Disclaimer*:**

The information provided in this book is as up to date and accurate as far as the author is aware. However, the subject matter covers areas that involve complex legal issues and rapidly evolving technology and businesses. This book is essentially based upon the UK market and associated laws and regulations. No liability is undertaken by the author or publisher for any losses incurred from individuals or others using the information herein. All readers are strongly recommended to seek professional advice in their own country before committing to any publishing activity or engaging in legal contracts.

To Aelred Tobin, who introduced me to print on demand which eventually led to me starting this book. Also to Bella Ingram, who gave me the inspiration and impetus to complete it.

CONTENTS

1. INTRODUCTION

This book has been written for authors who are considering self publishing using print on demand and/or e-books. In the modern digital age, it is important to consider alternatives to the traditional notion of an author submitting a manuscript to a large publishing company for consideration. Rejection is common, and yet there are many examples of such books achieving acclaim later. A manuscript may be judged to be of little merit, but does that mean it should never see the light of day? However, publishers are businesses that need to make money so they will only accept books that they expect will sell lots of copies. An author may have a different perspective although it is usually a nice prospect to reach a wide audience and receive a handsome reward! One such perspective is that the author has the right to publish their book if they are not relying upon others to fund the exercise. With the advent of new technology and on-line marketplaces, authors can self publish without using the established route and can exercise control over the whole process.

Most authors using traditional publishers do not get much support in terms of marketing and it is usually up to themselves to promote their books. Given that they can achieve higher returns per copy sold by self publishing, there is a serious question as to which might prove to be the most profitable option. This book provides a clear guide to the latest techniques, the advantages and disadvantages of self publishing and detailed information for authors considering this route.

Whilst it is possible for an author to undertake all of the tasks involved in publication, some use of the expertise and facilities of other parties is often necessary – not least in the process of printing and binding. But there are issues that some people find technically and procedurally onerous and authors often seek a mid-way solution by enlisting the services of others to assist them in producing their books. A convenient and inexpensive solution is to approach a small independent publisher who will undertake the various tasks and arrange for specialists to take care of services such as artwork, editing and proofreading.

The author may be lured by seemingly good offers on the internet where a book can be published for free or at a very low cost. These packages are usually minimal in the services provided, the financial returns are often low, and the author has few options in the overall process. A better alternative is that of assisted self publishing whereby companies offer services that free the author from the pitfalls and technicalities while allowing them control over important decisions. Such companies come with a variety of costs, extent and quality of service, financial returns and involvement of the author. After reading this book you will have a sound appreciation of the details of self publishing and an awareness of the benefits, or otherwise, of using professional and on-line services.

This book has been written by Steven Hodder of Takahe Publishing Ltd – a small, UK based company specialising in assisted self publishing for print on demand and e-books. It represents a collection of material that was originally prepared to support a personal consultation with the author at the start of the publishing process. The material has been extensively redrafted and extended to present a readable account and a permanent reference source. Apart from describing key features of the publishing process and sample details of available options, it also provides a physical example of a typical print on demand book.

There is no particular need to read this book in sequential order, although new authors are advised to read the next chapter giving an overview of the publishing process and the typical approach taken by self publishing authors and companies. It is important to understand the print on demand model and how it relates to other methods.

There is often confusion between terms such as *self publishing, assisted publishing, vanity publishing, subsidy publishing and print on demand.* These terms are clearly defined and explained in the next chapter of this book. It is important to understand these terms in the context of modern publishing and recent technology. The traditional publishing model based upon offset litho printing is not always the best option for today's authors and there are many situations where an alternative approach is more appropriate and more lucrative for the author. Conversely, there are situations where print on demand is not the best option and we shall try and give a fair and balanced treatment.

Much attention is given to the publication of e-books. An outline of the current technology and marketplace is given along with some considerations for production in this format, with or without an accompanying paper-based copy. The publication costs, pricing issues, and relative merits are discussed.

Other chapters include useful information for authors regarding typical print options, available trim sizes, and examples of costs and returns. Further information is given to enable the author to make informed decisions about setting the cover price, technical requirements for illustrations and photographs, and marketing and distribution.

This book also offers guidance relating to copyright, ISBNs, barcodes, and legal deposit libraries. Print on demand books will generally be available to the public through Amazon as well as being listed with major booksellers worldwide and instant printing in booksellers who use the Espresso Book Machine. But note that some retailers only recognise particular POD suppliers e.g. Lightning Source, when stocking books.

Most books in this genre have been written by American authors and some of the information is irrelevant or not applicable to readers outside the United States. This book attempts to consider the topic in a wider context and, whilst being based on a UK perspective, most of it is more generally applicable to a broader audience and we try to indicate where differences apply.

Authors can achieve a good amount of on-line sales using print on demand or e-books and, if successful, might receive an offer from a traditional publishing house. However, it might not necessarily be in their best interest to accept such an offer. With a clear knowledge of self publishing, the author can be in the best position to make decisions to maximise financial returns and achieve their goals.

This book is structured around the main issues relating to authors considering self publishing. As a consequence, there will be a little repetition of some basic information in different chapters where it is relevant to assist the overall readability. More detail of such information is given in the section to which it is most relevant.

It is hoped that this book will prove informative and useful. The information is as up to date as far as is reasonably possible at the time of writing, but readers are reminded that there are many factors subject to change e.g. prices, technology, legal issues, printing options and so on. It is important to check the latest details before committing to any self publishing options.

2. PUBLISHING OVERVIEW

Historical Perspective

The notion of publishing has been around since Roman times when slaves were trained to copy out manuscripts that would be offered for sale. The first mechanical printing presses appeared around 1440 and the mass production of books was widespread in Europe by 1500. Industrial scale printing was established in the 19th century with the advent of steam powered presses. The printing press works on the basis of pressure being applied to paper over an inked page of typeface. Early processes include lithography, in which the image is transferred to a waxy plate which is inked and pressed against the paper. Offset lithography, or more commonly, offset printing, rose to commercial popularity in the 1950s and remains as the most popular large volume printing technique. In this process the original image is transferred to the printing plate by inked rollers and then the printing plate transfers the ink to a rubber covered printing plate which, in turn, transfers the ink to the paper. Modern technology enables output from Desktop Publishing programs to directly output to the printing plate (computer to plate, CTP, imaging technology).

This form of publishing has been the basic model until relatively recently and large companies (publishing houses or publishers) have had control over not just the physical printing process but all other activities including commissioning, proofreading, editing, layout, paper selection, binding, cover design, marketing, warehousing and distribution. Modern companies now outsource some of these activities. The initial costs are high and a considerable outlay is required before a single copy is sold - and there is no guarantee that sufficient sales will be made to cover all these costs. Many publishers distribute books on a sale or return basis; sales that fall short of expectation need to be allowed for. Alternatively, books are offered at a deep discount on a non-return basis. Either way the potential revenue from a given book can be substantially reduced.

From the writer's point of view, the standard publishing model has its advantages and disadvantages. On the positive side, a manuscript that has been accepted by a major publisher is the first step on the ladder to fame and fortune. The author can sit back while the publisher's team of experts handle all the various tasks and maximise sales. On the negative side, a major problem is getting accepted. Many publishers will not accept unsolicited manuscripts and authors will generally require an agent who will expect a commission of 10-15%. For many years, there has been an alternative known as vanity publishing - a facility offered by certain small publishers that offer to print a number of copies of a book for a (usually substantial) up-front fee. Of course, these publishers did not use this name to describe their service but it was essentially a term of derision used by others to infer that the work was inferior and unlikely to be accepted by 'proper' publishers.

Of necessity, this introduction has been brief but the reader is referred to [8] for more details on the history and basics of publishing.

The Technological Revolution

Historically, the printing process was very labour intensive whereby type compositors physically created each page using moveable type. By the late 19th century the Linotype and similar machines helped automate the process using keyboard input. Today, the computer is a major feature in writing and publishing. Word Processing and Desktop Publishing are essential resources. We have already mentioned CTP technology in relation to offset litho printing and this is used extensively today for newspapers, magazines and books. Passing reference is also made to TeX and LaTeX, developed in the late 70s and early 80s, which are typesetting programs, the latter gained significant recognition, particularly in the mathematical world, for publishing scientific papers and books. By early 1980, minicomputers were being used for typesetting and the latter part of the decade saw the introduction of Desktop Publishing.

Other advances were also being made in the fields of printer technology. Laser and inkjet printers rapidly replaced those based upon typewriters (daisywheel printers). This enabled the computer user to select different fonts, styles, and sizes. Some activities associated with commercial printing companies were beginning to be in the hands of the individual. Certainly posters, leaflets and documents could be produced on a small scale and in colour. The writing process was transformed by the advances in word processing software including early dedicated word processing computers such as the Amstrad. Some authors resisted the changes (many still do!) but the advantages are numerous and can lead to a whole new approach to writing - particularly for those that have to produce documentation as part of their routine work.

An exciting spin-off from this revolution in printing and document creation came with the idea of *print on demand (POD)*. Modern laser printers are capable of producing small print runs of high quality and the process of bookbinding has evolved to offer automation. This is an alternative to traditional publishing and can be substantially cheaper when large quantities are not involved. The author can submit their manuscript in electronic format and it can be printed and bound for minimal cost.

Another facet of the revolution was the upsurge of the internet and on-line marketing. This has affected the book market strongly and with the extensive services of companies such as Amazon, book retailing has moved into another dimension with on-line sales of new and second-hand books from bookstores, individuals and, of course, Amazon itself (sometimes operating through other outlets).

With the widespread use of the internet in the 1990s came the rise of e-books (the availability of books in a readable electronic format). The origin of e-books is attributed to Project Gutenberg [16] that attempted to produce a wide variety of cultural works in plaintext and other formats. Advances in electronics enabled the development of small portable devices known as e-readers including the well known iPad and Kindle devices. There are still some compatibility issues with different file formats, but users can download from a great variety of choice at prices cheaper than printed versions or even for free. With the ability to store hundreds of books, they present an interesting addition to the market. Publishing for e-readers is on a par with print on demand and authors can offer books in both formats with relatively small initial costs.

Types of Self Publishing

To *Self Publish* is, according to [17], to 'publish (a piece of one's work) independently and at one's own expense'. This might imply that the self publishing author undertakes all aspects of the publishing processes including proofreading, editing, design, illustrations, layout, pricing, ISBN, printing, legal deposit, marketing, distribution, returns etc. These processes are described in further detail later in this chapter and elsewhere in this book.

In reality, a self publisher may well find it desirable or necessary to outsource some of these tasks to other agencies with expertise and/or specialist equipment. The most obvious example is the printing and binding of the books, but other services such as proofreading, editing and graphic design are also strong candidates.

It is therefore more realistic to refer to *assisted self publishing*, where the author chooses to use other parties in the publishing process, whilst retaining overall control. Some modern publishers offer a menu of services or even a comprehensive publishing package that frees the author from involvement with the technical minutiae and specialist activities whilst keeping them in control of major decisions.

There are different categories of self publishing (mainly vanity, subsidy, assisted POD and more recently e-publishing) but generally the author retains more control over the various processes and can receive a greater percentage of any profits. The different types of self publishing for printed books are briefly outlined below.

Vanity publishing is often a pejorative term that refers to the use of publishers that will accept any offering from an aspiring author and publish it at full cost to that author. Because this option arose in the times when traditional publishing was predominantly the only accepted way of getting into print, it gained its name through the notion that the work was of such little merit as to be unacceptable to the established publishing houses. Whilst there may be some truth in this, the stigma carries through to more modern times and can taint the perception of modern publishing methods such as POD even though most traditional publishers make use of this facility for certain categories such as back catalogues and initial print runs to establish demand. Vanity publishers typically offer no other services and may simply produce a printed and bound version of the original script - usually without assigning an ISBN. They may provide a book that appears to be a quality product, but it comes at a heavy price.

Subsidy publishing is similar to vanity publishing in that the author shares the costs usually with an up-front payment, but the publisher typically offers other services e.g. editing, layout, warehousing, marketing and distribution for which they bear the cost and, because they publish under their own imprint, they are more selective about what they accept. The author may not have much control over such factors as size, type, binding and cover design. The publisher maintains the rights over the book and pays royalties to the author. An example of such a publisher is Zeus Publications [18].

Assisted Print On Demand is a low cost publishing solution and is currently recognised as serious alternative for many authors. Usually, we are referring to a small publisher that offers a variety of services and forms the link between the author and the POD printers. Manuscripts can be submitted in a variety of formats including Word, HTML and PDF although high quality printing may necessitate the use of a professional package such as Adobe InDesign or perhaps a moderately priced Desktop Publishing program. Most POD publishers operate over the internet and offer packages that may include proofreading, editing, layout, cover design, ISBN, barcoding, and marketing. Some POD companies are connected with retail outlets e.g. Ingram Books and Amazon. There are POD printers, such as Lightning Source, that mainly deal with publishing companies as opposed to individual authors. However, they can offer significant marketing opportunities to those with specialist knowledge because book stores are prepared to carry their stock or accept customer orders.

Self Publishing Options for Authors

In the light of the above discussion, we turn our attention to the options available to the author who wants to self publish on a serious basis and generate some financial returns from their efforts.

1. Go it alone

Create your book, proofread, edit, do your own artwork, design your own cover, create your own title and verso pages with copyright, and permissions declarations, pages for dedications, acknowledgements, contents, index, etc. Assign an ISBN, barcode etc. Even print and bind your book and manage sales, distribution, stocking and returns.

This is all possible, but do you have all the expertise and equipment? Also, the whole process is going to be very time consuming - would you not be better off working on your next book?

2. Get some help

Most authors would not think of printing and binding their own work, so why not consider other services that can best be performed by professionals and that need not be of great cost. What about creating your book cover? Yes, we can all make a passable attempt at a cover image using one of the many software packages available, but do you really have the expertise? Be honest! Try creating one then, after a few days, go back to it and compare it to other book covers from your bookshelf – you may well be disappointed (or blind to the subtle creations of a good graphic designer).

Do you have suitable software to create your book's interior and cover? The internal layout needs to conform to the printer's requirements with consistent margins, layout and graphical content, if included. The printer will require digital files, usually Adobe PDF, that conform to strict standards – some of which are not attainable from standard 'publish as PDF' options available in most word processing programs.

Look through the details given in this book and decide what help you need and where you might look for it. Several on-line companies offer print on demand facilities with a selection of additional services, but you don't have much, if any, personal interaction. You have limited choices and you may have to charge a higher cover price than the market level. Financial returns tend to be lower than you could otherwise achieve.

When looking for assistance, particularly if you are looking for a complete self publishing package, also consider such factors as:

- How good and comprehensive is the service offered?
- Is it fixed-price or are there hidden extras?
- How much control do you have?
- What are the contractual arrangements?
- Can you pay in stages and when?
- Are there any ongoing costs?
- Who owns the rights to your book?
- Who sets the cover price and what are the restrictions?
- How do you get paid?
- How and where is the book available?
- What if you want to move publisher?
- How do you terminate the contract?

These and other issues will be dealt with more fully in the course of this book.

Summary of the Publishing Process

The following summary assumes that you are using the services of a publisher in assisting you to self publish your book for print on demand. Most of this is relevant even if you decide to undertake most of the work yourself. Further details can be found elsewhere in this book. This is only a guide - different publishers will have different approaches - but it is an indication of what can be expected.

Preliminaries: for self publishing, your manuscript needs to be complete or nearly so before you start looking for publishing services. Most people will have prepared their manuscript in word processed form, but if it is handwritten or typed, it will eventually need transcribing. Remember that this conversion will cost although typed text would usually involve less work because it can be scanned and passed through optical character recognition (OCR). You should be prepared to provide an outline of your proposed publication or some sample content when approaching a publisher so that they can assess whether it is feasible to publish your work and helps them to prepare for a personal consultation with you.

Personal consultation: this enables you and the publisher to get to know each other and to explore your requirements and intentions for the book. The various options will be discussed and the publisher will give you some idea of the costs and likely returns. They should also tell you about what they require and go through the main points of their publishing contract. Following the consultation, you should be provided with printed copies of any relevant documents and confirmation of the details of the understood requirements and expectations.

Submission of manuscript: when you have signed the publishing contract, you will probably be expected to pay part of the publishing fee and to supply your completed manuscript in a specified format within an agreed timescale.

Preliminary reading, verification, and approval: before proceeding with the publishing, a cursory reading of your manuscript would normally be undertaken to try and identify any major problems that might hinder or prevent publication.

Such problems might include unsuitable material or major editing requirements.

Proofreading and editing: an important part of the publishing process is *proofreading* where an experienced proof reader will attempt to identify any spelling or grammatical errors. Being human, the proof reader cannot absolutely guarantee the elimination of all errors, but will certainly be more effective than the author reading their own work. The proof reader may also advise on any editing requirements. An editor may be needed to advise you on any rewriting or restructuring that might be necessary.

Layout: once you and the publisher are mutually satisfied with the final manuscript, they can proceed to prepare the content for its final presentation. This will involve page layout, numbering, title pages, contents, etc. The final document will usually be in PDF format and compliant with the **PDF/X-1a:2001** standards required by the printers.

Cover price and discount: when the final page count is determined, it is possible to get an accurate pricing for the unit cost of the book that will be charged by the POD printers. This, in turn, enables a realistic cover price to be determined - bearing in mind that this must allow for a retail discount.

Cover design: the publisher will arrange for the professional design of the cover for your book in accordance with your wishes. Remember that the back cover will need some information and there will also be printing on the spine. Some aspects can only be completed when the final page count is determined and a template is used to lay out the front cover, the back cover and the spine.

First proof copy for approval: the publisher will provide you with the cover and internal content for your approval. At this stage, it may be in the form of two PDF documents in the final format. You should examine these carefully and inform the publisher of any problems or changes required. You may incur extra charges if you make changes once you have signed off the proof.

ISBN assignment: a book is uniquely identified by a 13-digit code - its ISBN (International Standard Book Number) - which will normally be assigned from the publisher's stock. This will appear on the inside of your book and on the back cover together with a barcode. You can also choose whether or not to display the book price along with these items. Any new edition of a book requires a new ISBN. For e-readers, an ISBN is not always necessary. When the publisher assigns an ISBN, they supply information about the book to the Nielsen ISBN Agency (in the UK) who, in turn, pass on this information to booksellers, libraries and other organisations worldwide. Their customers include Amazon.co.uk, Waterstones, WH Smith, Gardners, Bertrams, Askews Library Services, Play.com, and Blackwells.

Submission to printers: the publisher will submit your book to the POD printers in the form of separate digital files for the cover and the internal content. Normally, the print-on-demand printers can supply copies directly to customers thereby avoiding the problems of distribution, stocking, and returns. Books can also be supplied directly to the author who pays only for the printing and postage costs (subject to their contract with the publisher).

Final proof copy: the printer supplies the publisher with a proof copy of the printed book for final approval before it is released. However, the publishers are charged for changes either to the cover or to the content, so unless the problems arise through their own making, they may pass the charges on to the author if the changes arise there.

Legal Deposit: in the UK, there is a legal requirement for a copy of every published book to be submitted to the British Library. The publisher should send this copy as part of their service and they should also, if necessary, submit copies to the other five deposit libraries that are entitled to request a free copy of any book within 12 months of its publication. Further details can be found in chapter 7.

Marketing: Most publishers, for assisted self publishing, do not provide any services for marketing and distribution and these activities are generally the sole responsibility of the author. Some publishers will be happy to give some general advice and perhaps set up a web page for you and also advertise your book on their own website. Remember that most POD books will automatically be available on Amazon and so a judicious choice of title, sub-title and content summary will improve your visibility on searches. Most self publishing authors buy books directly at, or near, cost price and distribute these themselves. More guidance on marketing and promotion can be found in chapter 9.

3. MODERN TECHNOLOGY

Print on Demand

Since the mid 1990s, a new publishing process has evolved whereby books are printed as needed. This facility is known as print on demand (POD) and uses high quality laser printers to print books on a one copy at a time basis from stored electronic files. Whilst the norm is black and white printing, colour pages can be produced (although if the book is also offered in e-reader format, it should be noted that most readers are monochrome). POD printers are also now using ink-jet printers to enable colour books to be available at a more affordable price.

The print on demand model is as follows: a publisher submits the final form of a manuscript, usually in PDF format to the POD printer. It is accompanied by a separate file containing the cover design using a template supplied by the POD printer based upon details given beforehand e.g. trim size, page count. The printer checks that these files meet the required standards and transfers them to the computer system for their printing machines. The POD company is linked to distribution outlets such as booksellers, on-line retailers, book clubs etc. These outlets relay customer orders back to the POD company who print the required order and dispatch it to the distribution outlet. The books are then sent to the customers. The timescale is short enough to negate the need for stocks of books to be held at any stage.

It is important to distinguish between POD printers and POD publishers, although these are not always distinct entities e.g. Amazon operates a self publishing service called CreateSpace which, in turn, uses its own POD printing facilities. The author needs to know no more than the above outline of the POD model and the following discussion concentrates mainly on POD publishers.

A number of new companies have emerged that make extensive use of POD. These are mainly internet based and include some well-known names such as Lulu, Blurb, and CreateSpace (now incorporating Booksurge). Some of these companies offer a basic service for a low fee or even for free. However, the per-unit book supply cost is usually high and other services such as editing, layout, and cover design come at a not insignificant price. There is often a limited choice of print options such as paper quality, trim size and binding. Most POD-based publishers do not provide marketing or distribution facilities other than on-line sales – often through their own website. Few of these companies include proofreading, which is a specialist service and vital to the process; many new authors fail to appreciate that they are most unlikely to pick up their own mistakes. Another service that is generally not provided is that of editing whereby an experienced editor reviews the material and advises the author regarding changes to the text, structure, or content. A significant disadvantage of internet-based publishing companies is that there is little possibility for personal involvement. However there are companies that use POD and offer a range of services at a reasonable price while involving the author in significant decisions. Some of these companies provide all the main facilities as part of their standard publishing package at an affordable price and ensure close personal involvement with the author throughout the process.

POD technology is now widespread and is even used by traditional offset publishers for back catalogue books or those with a smaller market prospect. They also may use POD in the initial stages of publishing long-run books. On-line retailers such as Amazon make extensive use of POD although the purchaser is usually completely unaware of this fact. When a bookseller places an order, it is sent directly to the POD company e.g. Lightning Source, who print, bind, and ship the book back to the bookseller. From an author's point of view, this is attractive: the up-front costs are minimal, there are no costs for warehousing and distribution, no returns that have to be refunded. Against this, it should be said that the production cost per copy is higher but then a traditional publisher will have to set the retail price to include such factors as well as, perhaps, a higher discount that they give to the bookseller. Most POD publishers will not do the actual printing themselves, but will sub-contract that part of the process to a major POD company that handles the printing and binding. A well-known example is Lightning Source who deal mainly with publishers and expect a high degree of knowledge and expertise from their customers. However, they offer a 'no strings' service that will print and distribute a book for a fixed price and has automatic links to published book data. Major wholesalers and retailers have accounts with Lightning - the global distribution channels can be seen at [14] and for the UK these include Amazon, Bertrams, and Blackwells.

With POD or e-books, pricing, and hence royalties, are usually a matter for the author. This is good in the sense that the author can set the cover price to yield their expected percentage even though this may turn out to be unrealistic. That said, the use of a publisher that will actually enable a reasonable return, is an obvious requirement. An author may be drawn to Amazon Advantage - a service for small publishers which is open to authors who self publish. They offer to sell and distribute books but they charge 55% of the cover price, shipping costs, plus a small annual fee. If, however, the author publishes through Lightning Source, they can obtain a better return without the disadvantages. An up-front fee of around £100 covers a set-up fee for book and cover, a proof copy, an initial annual catalogue charge, with a bit left over towards possible amendments. The final cover price is determined by the printing cost plus the wholesale discount, plus the author's profit. For a typical 200 page paperback, the printing cost would be £2.70 and the wholesaler discount (determined by the author!) between 20% and 55% of the cover price. This means that a 200 page book with a cover price of £10 would give a return to the author of between £1.80 and £5.30 per copy sold. Further details, including a detailed discussion of discounts and cover prices, can be found in Shepard [5] and chapter 6 of this book.

An instant form of POD is available in some bookstores and small publishers via the Espresso Book Machine, invented in 1997. It offers the ability to print, bind and trim perfect-bound paperback books with full colour covers in under 4 minutes (for a 300 page book). It has automatic access to books from sources including Lightning Source and Google Books, offering over 3 million titles. Sheppard [5] sees some potential for the machine in international markets but points out that books published through Lightning Source will already be available by special order from domestic bookstores. The EBM brochure is available in PDF form from [13].

Publishing for e-readers

In recent years there has been a surge of interest in e-readers - small, portable devices that can download books, magazines, newspapers etc via a computer or using a wireless internet connection. The Kindle and iPad (although not a dedicated reader) are perhaps the best known because of the massive advertising campaigns, but these do not provide access to all e-book formats - discussed in more detail later in this section. Other readers such as Sony support different e-book formats and enable the user to acquire books from virtually any e-bookstore. An e-reader can also be another device such as a computer or an iPhone equipped with the relevant software.

Typical e-readers are about the size and weight of a paperback book and can be supplied with covers that give the look and feel of a real book. The traditional screen problem of diminishing visibility in bright light is overcome by using 'electronic ink' - the black and white elements of the display are physically altered and remain in place until a new page is required. This not only makes the page as readable as a normal page, but considerably saves power (an e-reader may not need recharging for up to a month). Some e-readers, such as the Kindle Paperlight also feature a built-in light for reading in dark conditions.

Other merits of the e-reader include the ability to store hundreds of books, instant dictionary definitions, bookmark and note facilities, and the ability to change the text size. The internet connectivity enables easy downloads of books and on-line subscription to newspapers. Many books are available for free download, others are usually lower priced than their printed counterparts. Whilst the storage capacity is good, there is still the facility with some companies such as Amazon, to delete a book on the device but to be able to retrieve it from your on-line stored books at a later date.

Most e-readers use the e-ink technology and are in black and white, although e-ink colour displays are starting to appear. The future is probably in colour as soon as the technology supports it at a reasonable price which, in turn, relies upon the increasing use of the e-reader and perhaps some standardisation in e-book format.

Kindle will only read its own AZW format as well as certain Mobi and PDF files. This may restrict the user to mainly Amazon as a source of e-books although there is a very large selection available here. An Amazon Kindle reader app is available for the iPhone and iPad. A source of free books that include Kindle versions is Project Gutenberg [16]. Probably the most popular e-book format used on other e-readers is epub which gives the user access to e-books from a wide variety of sources such as Project Gutenberg, Waterstones and W.H. Smith. Generally, e-readers will support more than one format including PDF and HTML files.

In order to prevent illegal copying, most e-books are protected by a DRM (digital rights management) system mostly using Adobe Digital Edition (ADEPT), compatible with most non Kindle e-readers. Note, however, that while the iPad supports epub it does not use the Adobe DRM so books bought from Apple's store can only be read on the iPad and not other e-readers. Similarly, e-books bought from other stores for other e-readers cannot be read on the iPad. We also note that the AZW format used by Kindle is the same as the mobi format but uses a different DRM system.

There is an important distinction between digital libraries and lending libraries. Digital libraries hold copies of books and other matter in digital format and these can be accessed via a computer network. Normal lending libraries have a facility for readers to access e-books and there are other facilities such as the Kindle Owners' Lending Library provided by Amazon.

When deciding whether to publish an e-book in addition to an existing printed version, the author should consider the effects of competition between these two versions and how this might affect on-line ratings. The increasing popularity of e-readers should not be ignored when choosing a publishing solution (or part of it). Colour versions will be more widely available within a few years and, along with the relentless advances in technology, e-readers will become a substantial marketplace for authors. Nevertheless, a printed version of a book will always be wanted but these two versions can be readily provided by publishers and, using print-on-demand for the hard copy, the overall costs can be minimised without diminishing the returns to the author.

When setting the price for an e-book, there are various factors to consider and these are covered in chapter 6. Note also that e-books are subject to VAT, unlike their printed counterparts, and this applies to sales in all EU countries. However, not all countries have adopted a minimum rate of 15%. Luxembourg has been charging a rate of 3% and France has been charging 7%. Amazon has been routing the sales of e-books through Luxembourg to take advantage of the lower rate. However, from 1st January 2015, VAT will be applied at the rate existing in the country to which the book is downloaded, so this will be 20% in the UK.

Creating an e-book

This section is, of necessity, only an outline. A full treatment could form a book in itself and, there is a good selection of such books available in both printed and e-reader formats as well as many good articles freely available on-line. Instead, we provide an overview of the process to give prospective e-authors a guide to what is required, some available resources, and the various options.

The basic requirements for an e-book don't really differ from those of a printed book. You need the main text of the manuscript, title page, copyright page etc. (see 'The Structure of a Book' in chapter 7). In either case, it is generally best to avoid any significant formatting in the early stages.

E-readers normally allow the user to change the font size for ease of reading. This means that the amount of text on any page is not fixed as in a printed book, so page numbers are not relevant. This, in turn, means that a table of contents or an index cannot use page numbering, but they will have to use hyperlinks instead if they are to be more than just lists.

Another issue is that of tables. If your manuscript contains tabular information, you will need to ensure that this will display correctly in an e-book. There are essentially two options: a simple formatted table, or an image of the table - both have their problems. In either case, the table must be of a size that can be displayed on the e-reader - and this, in itself can be quite restricting. If the table is a simple formatted table, remember to allow for the user to select different font sizes, as this will also affect the text in the table and may result in unwanted overflow. It may be better to use an image of the table which won't change size with font size changes. Sufficient resolution needs to be used so that the table is clear when displayed.

An e-book has its content stored in a collection of web-page type files (HTML or XHTML file format), usually with each chapter in a separate file. You will have probably created your manuscript using a word processor such as Microsoft Word and it is likely to be a single file. Your first task will be to split this up into separate files for separate chapters and other material e.g. the foreword. You can do this by copying and pasting into new documents. While you are doing this, remove any complicated formatting, choose a simple standard font and keep headings simple. For each of these new files, you want to create an HTML version. The easiest way of doing this is to use the 'Save As' facility and choose 'Web Page, Filtered' as the file type. The filtering should remove HTML tags that are unsuitable for e-readers although you might wish to use additional filtering software such as the free TagSoup program from: http://home.ccil.org/~cowan/XML/tagsoup/.

You've now got your content organised and ready for the next step of putting together your e-book. This can be done manually, but there is quite a lot to learn and there are many pitfalls. It is generally easier and quicker, at this stage, to use some purpose built software. What you use will depend upon whether you wish to create an epub book for general readership or a mobi file for the Amazon marketplace.

Let's start with an epub book. There is a very nice, free piece of software called Sigil available at:

https://code.google.com/p/sigil/

with versions for both Windows and Mac OS. It is supported by a clear user guide that can be viewed on-line or downloaded as an epub book. The guide contains tutorials that take you through the steps in using the program to create your e-book and the program is easy to use while offering all the facilities you need. Epub books can be read using Adobe Digital Editions which is freely available as a download from:

http://www.adobe.com/uk/products/digital-editions/download.html

To create a mobi e-book you can also use freely available software. The Mobipocket Creator can be downloaded from www.mobipocket.com along with the Mobipocket Reader. For the Creator, there is a choice between the Home edition and the Publisher Edition, both are free; choose the Publisher edition with its additional file import facilities. Using the program is fairly simple and intuitive and it comes with a useful help file that gives clear instructions for creating your mobi e-book.

Although the do it yourself approach is quite straightforward, you may prefer to get somebody else to create your e-book for you. There are conversion houses that will take your manuscript and produce an e-book in your selected format(s) or you could use the services of an independent publisher. In the latter case, you might get the benefit of additional services such as proofreading, editing, ISBN assignment, and cover design. Even if you don't include a cover image in your e-book, you will need a colour image for advertising and sales purposes. If you just want to create an e-book in mobi format for Amazon, you can just send them your original Word files and they will do the conversion for you. Kindle Direct Publishing:

https://kdp.amazon.com/self publishing/signin

is worth considering if you are looking for a straightforward way to produce and publish your e-book. The website contains a simplified guide to creating the required files and what they expect - it's worth reading even if you don't intend to use the service. Go to the above website and click 'Get Started' and look for the link to the simplified guide. Also see chapter 10 of this book.

4. SELF PUBLISHING

Why Self Publish?

In chapter 2, we introduced some terms associated with different types of self publishing. It will be useful to establish a definition of self publishing for the purposes of our discussion, so we offer the following:

Self Publishing is the publication of a book by the author, at their own expense, with or without using additional professional services.

The key point here is that the author is the one who decides to publish and is not reliant upon acceptance from a publisher. The author will generally engage the services of others in order to complete the publication even if this is only a company that prints and binds the books. Other services might include artwork, editing, layout, proofreading, ISBN and barcoding, marketing and distribution. These services cost money and the author can expect to pay any such fees up front. While there are websites that offer to publish your book for a minimal cost or even for free, remember that you don't get anything for nothing and such services are basic and supply costs are often high.

The above definition and remarks also apply to e-books and many authors are choosing to self publish solely in this medium. Creating and publishing an e-book can be relatively simple and inexpensive. Technical details can be found in chapter 3 of this book and some further notes appear later in this chapter.

There are a number of reasons why an author might choose to self publish and these include:

- Higher returns per copy sold
- Control over all decisions
- Retention of all rights
- Ability to switch publishers
- No stocking, distribution, or returns costs
- Easy access to a worldwide market
- Ability to buy books at cost and sell locally
- Easy access to specialist publishing services

We don't dismiss the role of major publishing houses that have the potential to rocket an unknown author to the best sellers list and beyond. But, being realistic, few authors reach these dizzy heights and many are rejected with little consideration.

There are also authors who are creating works for which there are a limited number of possible customers, but know that their work will be well received amongst this target market. Such works include local and family histories, poetry collections, short stories, club and society histories and achievements, personal diaries and recollections, interesting takes on life, etc.

Whilst we identify non-fiction authors as an obvious sector for self publishing, there are opportunities for first-time authors of fiction to establish their credibility in the book market without the humiliation of countless rejections (J.K. Rowling's first Harry Potter book was rejected many times!)

Why not test the market first with an e-book – it need not cost anything! If your book sells well, then you might attract the attention of major publishers (but you still might be better off by self publishing!)

Finally, don't be put off by people who dismiss this as 'vanity publishing'. Self publishing is a viable alternative in the present age where new technology and on-line sales are having a serious impact on established publishing houses. Yes there are some bad examples of self published work, but that doesn't mean that all self published books are inferior. There are also many book categories where self publishing represents the best option e.g. where the target audience is limited. Also, even big publishers use print on demand when it is convenient for them.

Becoming a Publisher

It is not necessary to set up a publishing company in order to self publish and, for most authors, this would be unlikely to be a serious option. However, for some, setting up their own publishing company might be an attractive proposition.

As a publisher, you have a better status than a lone author and there could be financial benefits if you publish and sell several books. Also, some companies, such as Lightning Source, mainly only deal with publishers and they are a major print on demand organisation.

Basically, in the UK, there are three types of business: sole trader, partnership, and limited company. Being a sole trader is probably the simplest option but the three options are briefly outlined below. Whichever you choose, it is probably worth having a chat with an accountant first and you will need their services later. They probably won't charge you for initial advice because they want your business! Try and find an accountant by recommendation from other traders or companies – the cost and helpfulness can vary considerably. For UK businesses, the National Business Register (http://www.start.biz/home.htm) may be a useful reference, especially for sole traders. We first take a brief look at the different types of business and then give an overview of the common factors that every prospective business needs to consider.

Sole Trader

This is the most basic type of business and a popular choice for many people. Essentially, you choose a name and start trading. You must register with HMRC within the first three months. You are not required to keep accounts by law, but you will need them for tax purposes. However, your accountant will charge you less than for a limited company. Also, you are not liable for corporation tax. It is useful, but not essential, to have a separate bank account from your own current account. A separate account enables your business to have an entity of its own and greatly simplifies things – especially with your accountant.

Every business needs a name. Many sole traders use their own names or include their name in the title e.g. Jack Jones Publishing, however you can use titles that don't refer to your name e.g. Landslip Publishing as long as you don't misrepresent your function or status. You also need to check that your chosen business name does not coincide with an existing business where there could be confusion. You may not use 'limited', 'ltd', or 'plc' as a sole trader. Some traders also wonder what they can use for their own job title e.g. on business cards and in correspondence. The title 'proprietor' is usually chosen, although 'manager' or 'owner' could be appropriate. The use of 'director' is permissible although this is a term associated with limited companies and might be a little misleading. For a publishing business, the term 'publisher' might be the simplest choice.

A disadvantage of being a sole trader is that, legally, you and the business are not distinct – even if you have a separate bank account for your business. So if the business loses money or becomes subject to some major financial calamity, you are responsible for the costs! As a publisher, you could be exposed to some risk if you inadvertently publish material that is plagiarised, defamatory, offensive, obtrusive, or contentious in some other way. We discuss these risks elsewhere in this book, how to avoid them, and how to mitigate the possible damages. However, as a sole trader, such a problem could destroy your publishing business and make you personally bankrupt! You might get some protection from some professional insurance, but ultimately you bear the final responsibility.

Another potential disadvantage is that if you eventually want to sell your business, should it become successful, you might find it more difficult than selling a limited company due to its legal status.

Partnership

A partnership is similar to a sole trader except that it involves two or more people. It has the same advantages and disadvantages and has no legal status. Partners should draw up a legal agreement governing their responsibilities and respective liabilities (although they cannot abrogate the overall liability of the partnership).

A variation on this is a 'Limited Liability Partnership' (LLP). It has a legal entity and requires registration with Companies House. Each partner should be registered with HMRC as self-employed. There is a need to file detailed accounts which inevitably means higher accountancy fees. The partners are protected to some extent from individual liability for losses although they might be sued for negligence.

A partnership would generally need to set up a separate bank account even if this was, say, a husband and wife enterprise with a joint current account. Keep business and personal accounts separate – it makes life a lot easier!

Limited Company

A limited company is formed from one or more people, known as *directors*. It is a legal entity in which there is a distinct separation of the company and its directors with regard to the financial liabilities. There must be at least one director and, until recently, there was a requirement to have a Company Secretary who had a responsibility to ensure that all returns were submitted in accordance with the legal requirements. Whilst this role is no longer obligatory, it could be useful to appoint someone in this capacity who might take on responsibility for other administrative duties so that the director(s) can concentrate on the everyday, customer-based, aspects of the business.

It is easy to set up a limited company. As we have said before, if you are thinking about going into business, arrange a free chat with an accountant first. They can set up the company for you, although you can do this yourself online much cheaper! Have a look at the Companies House website (all UK limited companies must register with Companies House) you will find all the information there and you can register your company for a very modest fee with the minimum of fuss. Beware! Once you register, you will be inundated with all sorts of tempting offers for finance, offices, support etc. Just ignore them and plough your own furrow!

With the status of a limited company, you will want a business bank account. This might seem intimidating because you may feel you are asking for some sort of credit without credentials! Fear not! Banks desperately want your business and they will offer generous (?) terms for those who will sign up with them. If you're not looking for initial finance or credit they will readily open a business account for you and probably offer a business credit card with about a £1,000 limit for some 'working finance'. It's good to go armed with a business plan so that you can demonstrate that you have given some serious thought to your venture and that you are a worthwhile risk to them. Many banks have a template for a business plan to download. They will carry out credit checks before they give you an account or loans, but they will usually do this online while you wait.

There are several advantages of establishing a limited company: status when dealing with other companies and institutions, limited liability, easier ways to raise funds, etc. On the other hand, there are more onerous requirements for registration, accounts, annual returns, and paying corporation tax. Accountancy fees are higher than those for a sole trader because there are more stringent regulations placed on a limited company.

Should you register for VAT?

The option to register for VAT is available to limited companies, partnerships and sole traders. Although you are obliged to register if your annual turnover is in excess of £81,000 (as at June 2014), you can elect to register on lower turnovers. While printed books are zero rated, e-books are subject to VAT and there may be advantages in registering. If you are providing a publishing service, your customers would incur VAT on the charges for your services, but you could reclaim VAT on the various monies that you pay out. For a small publishing company, this is unlikely to be worthwhile considering the extra costs to your customers and the need to complete regular returns and keep detailed records.

Other Considerations

If you are publishing books for other authors you will need to consider your potential liabilities in the event of publishing contentious material. You can protect yourself, to some extent, by drawing up a comprehensive legal contract that places as much onus upon the author as is possible and sets out your strategy should a legal challenge being mounted. We look at these issues and other legal matters in further detail in chapter 8. Also, in a related way, there is the question of business insurance. It may well be worth taking out professional indemnity insurance to protect yourself against claims from people who consider that they have been libelled by one of your authors or have otherwise suffered as a result of publication e.g. breach of privacy, breach of copyright, or psychological injury. Also, if you invite clients to your premises, then you should take out suitable insurance to cover safety issues.

Software and Hardware Requirements

As a publisher, you will need various software and hardware facilities. Surprisingly, this does not have to cost you much to get started. Hardware facilities can be basically fulfilled by a suitable computer and multi-function printer. Most software is freely available as online downloads, although you will probably need Microsoft Word and a reasonably capable publishing package such as Microsoft Publisher or Serif Page Plus (available at a very reasonable price). In the following, we take a brief look at the various items of software that you might require.

Word Processor: If you are publishing for other authors it is useful, although not essential, if you can load their manuscripts into your word processor for proofreading and editing. As most people use Microsoft Word, it makes sense to have this program yourself and the other programs that come with the Office suite are very useful. If Microsoft Office is beyond your budget, consider using Apache Open Office which is available as a free download from http://www.openoffice.org/ - the word processor will open a variety of documents and has more than enough features to allow you to carry out your work. If you are going to publish e-books, your word processor needs to be able to save documents in web page form (html) with some filtering to remove certain tags that may cause problems with e-readers. A useful option in this respect is the Atlantis Word Processor available from http://www.atlantiswordprocessor.com/en/ for about £22 and you can try it out for free on a 30 day trial period. The program outputs 'clean' html and will create both epub and kindle books. Their website also gives detailed instructions for creating e-books using the word processor.

Desk-top Publisher: When publishing for printed books, a good desk-top publishing program is very useful. Printers normally require files in PDF format for both content and cover and they will want these to comply with the PDF X1a standard. Although many word processors will export to PDF, they do not necessarily offer the required compliance. A useful, but not essential, tool to accompany this would be Adobe Acrobat. While the reader is free, the program for creating and manipulating PDF files is fairly expensive - particularly the professional edition. As mentioned, Serif software offer acceptable alternatives at budget prices.

Picture Editing Software: Most people already possess some form of picture editing software for use with their digital cameras. There are many good programs available and a lot are free or come packaged with other products. Most of these will interact with a scanner and offer a range of editing options. It is useful to be able to resize pictures e.g. to alter an existing image to a standard cover image for an e-book (600 x 800 pixels).

Graphics/Drawing Software: It is convenient to have a suitable graphics program that fills the gap between desktop publishing and picture editing. There are many low-cost or even free programs available and it is useful to have one that can import and export PDF files. A program that enables you to work with layered images is particularly useful when creating book covers using a design template (see later in this chapter).

Software for e-books: In chapter 3, we gave an overview of the process of creating an e-book and mentioned the software requirements. Briefly, for Kindle books, you will want Kindlegen and Mobipocket Creator which are available as free downloads. Note that if you are using the Atlantis Word Processor, mentioned above, you still require Kindlegen to be installed on your computer. For epub books, we considered Sigil (also free) or you could again use the Atlantis Word Processor.

Accountancy Software: If you are running your own business, you need to keep accounts and you may find it useful to use some dedicated software for this purpose. Your accountants will probably use Sage software, so you might save a little on their bills by using a simple version in this range. However, some accounting programs are complicated and assume some basic accountancy knowledge so you may want to use everyday software to keep your records. Most accountants are quite happy to receive an Excel spreadsheet and you can use different worksheets to record different details e.g. bank account, sales, purchases etc.

Technicalities

As a publisher, you need to have a clear idea of the processes involved between receiving a manuscript and submitting the required files to the printers. Or if you are offering to publish e-books, you will need to know how to convert the original manuscript into the required format and how you submit it for publication. Some of these details are covered elsewhere in this book but in this section we shall outline the main activities involved and refer you to other sections for further details.

Whether you are dealing with a printed book or an e-book, there are many common activities that you, as the publisher, need to undertake. On receiving a manuscript, you will need to ensure that the content is suitable for publication - this covers many issues relating to originality, quality, and suitability. You will probably need to engage the services of professionals for such aspects as proofreading, editing, and artwork, although you can do some preliminary work yourself. You should beware of badly written manuscripts or dubious material. Such problems can be easily detected with a preliminary read-through and you can save yourself a lot of hassle by rejecting obvious problem manuscripts. Assuming that everything looks reasonable, you can proceed with the other aspects of publishing such as assigning an ISBN, arranging a publication date, commissioning artwork, and agreeing the descriptions for the back cover and advertising material. More details on these issues can be found elsewhere in this book, but we try to outline the main points in the following discussion.

What's involved in creating a book ready to send to POD?

At an early stage, you can assign an ISBN to the forthcoming book and set a publication date. Assuming that, as a publisher, you have purchased a block of ISBNs, you need to allocate one of these to the book and notify the details to the relevant ISBN agency. For the UK, this is Neilsen and they will have given further details with your allocation or you can check with their website. You will be required to submit various details of your book at this time including a brief description, the publication date and the cover price.

Once the manuscript has been proof read and edited, it will need to be converted to PDF format and compliant with the PDF X1a standard. Before you do the conversion, ensure that your original manuscript has been suitably prepared for the final page size, margins, and page numbering. This might be done in Word, but probably better to import your document into your desktop publishing program and do the necessary formatting in there. Page numbers need special consideration as there may be discontinuities between sections of a book and they may not be present in all parts. Further details can be found in chapter 7 of this book. This is also the time to check out problems where paragraph breaks have occurred with page boundaries resulting in a line space at the top of a page. Once you have double-checked for all problems, do the conversion to PDF and make sure that any warnings are resolved. You should also check through the final PDF document in case there are other problems. When you are satisfied that this final version is all right, give a copy to the author as a proof for approval. It is important that you get approval at this stage because although the printers will produce a proof copy for you (at a cost), they will charge you for any subsequent amendments to the text or the cover.

The cover design can be done at any stage but it is best not finalise this until you have the final PDF version signed off by the author. You will then know the exact number of pages involved and you can download a cover template from the printers that is specific for that number of pages. This template will be a PDF document with lines for boundaries and cropping marks. The boundary lines are for your guidance when positioning the text and images that form the front cover, back cover and spine. These lines should not show on the final PDF file that you submit as your cover, but other marks should remain. You will need some suitable graphics software to create your cover using the template. This does not have to be expensive, but it should be able to import PDF files, support layers and export PDF to the required standard. An affordable program that offers all the necessary facilities is Serif Draw Plus and although the latest version is X6, you should be able to buy an earlier version cheaply or use the free starter edition. Don't forget to check the final PDF file for the cover in some detail. I once had to revise a cover when the proof copy of a book showed some red dots on the cover that were residuals of the corners of deleted borders from a template. They didn't show up in the artwork prior to generating the PDF but they did appear in the final PDF file and I hadn't spotted them!

You now have your two PDF files: one for the content and the other for the cover. These can now be uploaded to your POD printer and you'll soon be in print. It's a good idea to order a proof copy just in case any problems have slipped through, in which case you can make any revisions before the book is available to the public.

Once the book is published, there is a requirement to send one copy to the British Library and you can send copies to the other legal deposit libraries. For further details, see chapter 7.

What's involved in creating an e-book and making it available?

The details of creating and publishing an e-book vary somewhat according to the type of book and where it will be marketed. Basically, the alternatives are an e-pub book for the general market or a mobi book for the Amazon Kindle market. We provide an overview of the technicalities in chapter 3, so we will not repeat these here.

Much of the preparatory work is the same as for a printed book, other than you want to prepare a set of minimally formatted, word-processed files for the different chapters of the book. You then save these in a filtered HTML format from which the e-book can be constructed. The need for careful proof reading remains as does the need for the author to sign off a proof copy at some stage.

It is a good idea to assign an ISBN to the e-book even if you don't strictly need one. Remember to assign different ISBNs to each different e-book format used. Amazon doesn't insist on an ISBN as they assign their own identification to the book.

You will need a cover image for the e-book. This should be 600 x 800 pixels and it can be used both as an internal image in the e-book and as an advertising image for the e-bookshop. A colour image is best - although check that it still looks presentable when converted to greyscale. You will also need to prepare a table of contents that can simply identify the different chapters of the book.

If you are publishing an e-book for the general market in the epub format, you can assemble your e-book with a program like Sigil (see chapter 3) and check the final version with a suitable e-reader or computer program such as Adobe Digital Editions. You then need to submit your epub book to your chosen market(s). One option is to sell direct from your own website. You can set this up fairly simply using a Paypal account and some means of permitting downloads. You would also need some fairly sophisticated search engine optimization to drive traffic to your website. An alternative, or perhaps an addition, would be to get the main e-book sellers such as W.H. Smith, Barnes & Noble and so on, to stock your book.

Alternatively, if you are creating a mobi file for the Amazon marketplace you could use software such as MobiPocket Creator or submit the HTML files directly to Kindle Direct Publishing.

Assisted Self Publishing

If you are an author and, having read the guidance in this book, you have decided that you would like to self publish but would prefer that someone else sorted out all the details, you should approach an independent publishing company that can handle all the issues for you - although it will cost you a small fee. The benefits of this service can be invaluable to the author who just wants to write and not be involved with the technicalities of self publishing and yet enjoy the benefits therein. Alternatively, you might be a successful self published author who sees an opportunity to supplement your income by using your expertise and spare time to assist other authors to self publish. Even if you are not a writer yourself, you might want to set up a publishing business so that other writers can self publish and you supply the expertise and resources to enable them to do this at an affordable price.

Whatever, the situation regarding your personal involvement, we have the concept of assisted self publishing whereby a writer can access the necessary resources to get their book published at a reasonable price and for it to be available on-line or supplied 'direct to author' at or near cost price. The writer should be able to elect for a printed book, an e-book, or both. A key aspect of this is that it is the writer who chooses to publish, when to publish, and what resources they need to achieve this.

One benefit of assisted self publishing is that the author is in control and not at the behest of some large publishing house. While the volume of sales might be smaller, the returns per copy are significantly greater - but the writer should check out the exact details of the deal before engaging the services of an independent publishing company. There are many writers who would like to self publish but are put off by the technicalities involved and, for them, the option of engaging publishing services is an attractive alternative. A good publisher offering such services will have the expertise, software and resources to make this a useful facility and they can offer a comprehensive publishing package for a price that is well worth the hassle avoided. The writer's time is best spent writing!

Of course there are pitfalls in the process of assisted self publishing or even self publishing. You need to be sure that you really want to self publish in the first place. Are you aware of what this really entails? If you are not sure, please read the rest of this book first! Consider the genre of your book and the target audience. Who is going to buy it and do they want it in printed or electronic form? How many people will be interested in it? Is it a potential blockbuster novel or is it a specialist book with a limited audience? What are you seeking to gain from the publication? If you give these points serious consideration, you should be able to gauge whether to approach a major publishing house or to self publish.

One of the most common problems with self publishing is the quality of the final product - particularly with e-books, but not uncommon with printed versions. The most common problems are typos (and other spelling mistakes), poor punctuation, grammar, and a lack of editing. Your reputation as a writer - and hence your future sales - can be severely damaged at the outset by publishing a book with some of these problems. This is where assisted self publishing can be worth its while because a good company will offer services such as proofreading and editing and give you a final product that won't antagonise readers! However good you think you are, it is well worth getting an experienced person to review your material - the writer is usually the last to spot any structural problems and will often overlook spelling errors.

Using assisted self publishing services inevitably comes at a cost and you have to balance the benefits against the time, effort and resources involved if you were to undertake all the tasks yourself. There are many factors to consider - take, for example, the need to assign an ISBN to your book. As an author wanting a single ISBN you will pay significantly more because you will need to purchase a block of at least 10 ISBNs even if you never intend to publish another book! Using the services of a small publisher will save you money on the ISBN because they will have purchased a large block of ISBNs for a considerably lower unit price. The benefit on the ISBN is probably only a small gain, but when you consider other services such as proofreading, editing, and artwork, your publisher can probably save you a lot of money by using professional contacts with whom an agreement has been made that ensures them regular work albeit for a smaller fee.

To sum up, the writer is advised to seriously consider using the services of an independent publisher if they can offer the right package for the right price. It is a moderate outlay for publishing a book but, when you consider what you can get and the ability to hand over to someone that knows what they are doing and will take care of all the details, there is a strong case for assisted self publishing. There is a great temptation for all self publishing authors to take their newly finished manuscript and publish it straight away - unfortunately, the ease with which books can be published often results in many sub-standard books being offered for sale. This situation is to the benefit of no-one; if an author or publisher gains a bad reputation for sub-standard material, they will not sell many copies and will struggle to regain their reputation. Quality has to be a key byword and the writer must realise that the completion of the manuscript is not the completion of the book - but this is the point that one hands over to assisted self publishing in order to complete the project at the right price, for the right quality and for the best returns.

Summary

This chapter has looked at the idea of self publishing and indicated what you need to do in order to self publish your book. We have considered the advantages and disadvantages of self publishing and the potential benefits of engaging the services of an independent publisher. Attention has been given to e-books as well as the printed version, but the writer should give careful consideration to the potential readership before committing to any given form and also decide whether self publishing is the best option.

5. USING THE SERVICES OF A PUBLISHER (ASSISTED SELF PUBLISHING)

In this chapter we consider the merits of using publishing services from an author's point of view. What services can you expect to be offered and are any of these optional? How much is it likely to cost and what are the payment options? What is the legal relationship between you and the publisher? In what form does your publisher expect to receive your manuscript? What choices can you expect to have regarding book size and type? What degree of personal involvement do you have in the publishing process? This chapter starts with the notion of publishing a printed book and although many aspects also apply to e-books, we conclude with a look at the particular considerations related to publishing an e-book.

Approaching a Publisher

You have completed your manuscript and you have decided to self publish, but you want someone to do the technical bits for you - while you remain in control. So your first task is to find an independent publisher who will take care of all the details while keeping you in the loop and giving you the final say on all important decisions. Also, they need to be able to offer the range of services that you require and at a price that you can afford. Your first step is to find that publisher and it is important that, before you start your search, you make a realistic appraisal of your own skills, limitations, expectations and budget.

Publishing does not have to be a costly exercise, but the more activities and resources that you require will inevitably increase the price. However, it is not worth cutting corners and ending up with a second rate publication. Spend time to find a publisher that you can work with to the level that you require and give careful consideration to any advice offered.

Should you use one of the low-cost, do it yourself internet sites or engage the services of a local publisher? You can find further details of internet services later in this book, but they do require some degree of technical ability, choices are limited, personal contact is minimal and the final cover prices are generally high with small returns for the author. For a little extra outlay you could find a publisher who will perhaps read your book, give you advice, discuss options with you and, most importantly take care of all the publishing details while you get on with writing your next book!

Most publishers will have their own website or registration in local business listings. If you don't have your own internet access, you can always visit your local library and use their services. The library staff will be available to assist if you are not familiar with computers. Do a search for publishers in your area, look at their websites and see what they have to offer. Also, make a list of the telephone numbers of likely publishers and give them a call - but prepare your questions first to save time and money. The rest of this section will help you to sort out what you should be asking.

Range of Services and Options

Before approaching a publisher, you should be clear about the services and options that you are expecting so that you can ensure that they will be able to fulfil your wishes and at a suitable price. As your initial contact is likely to be by telephone, prepare some details and basic questions. Your publisher will probably want some initial background information such as what your book is about, what size is it, what stage are you at, what are your publishing goals etc. You will probably want to ask about costs, timescale, required format of manuscript, how much you are involved and so on.

It may also be useful to look at an example of a book that has been published by them - it might not be on the bookshelves of your local store but, at least, you can ask them to show you something when you first meet them.

A great advantage of using the services of a publisher is that you have personal contact with them and they should be able to offer you an initial meeting in which you can discuss your requirements in some detail and establish a working relationship. You might expect to pay a small fee for this personal consultation, but this should be refundable towards the cost of publishing if you decide to proceed. It is only reasonable for a publisher to make a small charge for providing a few hours of their time for meeting you and discussing, in detail, the options for publishing your book. Equally, you can expect to get something useful out of this meeting. An important aspect of this is that your publisher should understand exactly what you want and that they talk through all the options available to you. You should have a clear idea of exactly what you will get, what it will cost, what you can expect in returns, what are the timescales, and what are the payment schedules on both sides. Also, you should be able to see a sample contract that you can take away and study before you sign up.

Apart from the essential publishing process, your publisher should be able to offer the services of proofreading and editing. The wise author doesn't dismiss these because of the extra costs and any person is conceited if they believe that their original manuscript is free from errors and could not benefit from the critical eye of a professional. At least consider some basic proofreading - it is all too easy to read through your own script without spotting inadvertent typos.

Costs and Payment Options

With regard to costs, it is well to remember the old adage 'you get what you pay for'. If you are engaging the services of a publisher, they will charge for their time plus any costs involved e.g. set-up and catalogue costs with a POD printer, ISBN assignment, artwork, legal deposit etc. So, if someone offers to publish your book for 100 pounds then you are either not going to get very much for your money or you won't get much in the way of returns on a high cover price - or both!

You will inevitably have to balance the cost of publishing with the level of returns that you can expect. On the one hand, a more expensive publishing package could give you the full returns from sales and, on the other hand, a cheaper package will yield lower returns per copy sold and the publisher might demand a higher cover price. Also, as a self publisher, you will want to sell copies directly yourself - so you need to be able to obtain these copies at, or near cost price - check this out before you sign up!

Legal Issues

Before you engage the services of a publisher, it would be wise to consider some legal issues because you will be signing a legally binding contract and you should have a good idea of what you should be looking out for. You will need to be aware of your responsibilities e.g. originality, content, rights and your publisher's responsibilities e.g. timescale, rights, legal deposit.

As we have already mentioned, ask for a sample contract in your initial meeting and read it through at your leisure. What should you look for in a legal contract? You are referred to chapter 8 for a detailed discussion of typical issues covered in a contract, but this section outlines the legal relationship between you and your publisher.

With regard to your responsibilities, you have a duty to assert your ownership of the material that you are publishing and that you can give your publisher an assurance that there are no known reasons for legal action against your publication. If the work is original, you should avoid reference to identifiable persons or companies and institutions. You should be particularly careful to avoid potentially libellous or contentious issues - if in doubt, leave it out! Also ensure that you give full acknowledgement to any sources that you use - seek permission if you are not sure. If the work is a republication, make sure that you have the full rights to republish and expect the publisher to ask you for the evidence!

Your publisher also has various responsibilities and it is worthwhile checking what they are prepared to commit to in the contract. While most of the details relate to the minutiae of publication, you should ensure that you are not signing away your rights. However, you will be granting licence of your copyright on a temporary basis. The contract should contain details of financial arrangements and provisions for termination of contract e.g. if you choose to issue a future edition with another publisher. There should also be provision for dispute resolution and this is as much in your interest as the publisher's.

Trim Sizes and Options

Standard book publishing packages for print on demand use a set range of trim sizes, binding options and choice of paper. Specific details of what your publisher can offer can be found out when you meet and discuss your requirements, but a general outline is given below. Different options may be available according to whether the book has a colour or black and white interior.

A number of trim sizes are typically available from around 5 x 8 inches (127 x 203 mm) up to 8.5 x 11 inches (216 x 280 mm). The choice of trim size has some bearing on the print cost that is based upon a cost per page and a unit cost. For black and white interiors, the trim size does not greatly change the overall cost but for colour interiors, this may be a significant consideration.

A choice of binding is usually available for all books although the actual options may depend on the trim size and number of pages. The basic choices are: saddle-stitch, perfect bound (for paperbacks), case laminate (hard covers) and blue or grey cloth covers. Books can be supplied with jackets for certain options.

Most options use white 75gsm paper although cream 85gsm paper may be available for some black and white interiors. A heavier paper can reduce the problems of 'show through' where the contents of a page can be slightly visible on the reverse - this can be troublesome on light portions of an image.

One other consideration is whether the interior should be in colour or black and white, although this is often dictated by the nature of the book itself. Colour interiors usually represent a significant increase in the production cost of the book and may make it prohibitively expensive for those with a large number of pages. Some printers are able to offer a cheaper colour alternative by using inkjet technology instead of the usual laser printers. So for a book with around 50 pages, a colour interior may not cost any more than a black and white one.

Personal Involvement

If you are using the services of a publisher, you will expect them to take care of all the technical aspects, but you will want to be involved in any significant decisions. When you make an initial enquiry to see if there is a realistic prospect of publishing with a particular publisher, ask about the level of personal involvement that you will have in the process. This first occurs when you meet your publisher to discuss your book, the various options open to you, and such issues as cost and timescale. Your next involvement will probably be when the publisher sends a written summary of the discussion and decisions reached together with a draft contract. You will be asked to check these documents carefully, give written confirmation of the options, to sign the contract and to pay all or part of the publishing fee.

Your publisher should be able to design the book cover in accordance with your wishes or you might want to provide your own cover; this should be discussed in your initial personal consultation. If the publisher provides the design, you should be able to approve this before publication. As part of the cover design, there will be text on the back cover and you should be involved in agreeing what is provided. Similarly, you should be able to see and approve any images and text that will be used for on-line marketing.

Some publishers offer a dedicated webpage for your book as part of the publishing package although you might be asked to contribute to the web hosting and domain name fees after the first year or so. A draft version should be supplied to you for approval before going live. The website is probably as much as the publisher offers in respect of marketing since this is essentially still 'self publishing'. Some publishers might offer some marketing advice or perhaps arrange a book launch event for you.

A copy of the book will be supplied to you, usually in PDF format, for checking and approval. This is an important stage because you are approving the final version of the book that will be submitted for printing. Any changes after this stage may incur a fee as there are charges made by the printers for submission of revised content or cover.

The publishers will obtain a proof copy of the book prior to the release of the book. This will be checked by the publishers and you will be asked for final approval. Changes will be probably be subject to fees as described above unless the problems are attributable to the publisher or the printers.

Following publication, you will probably not have much further contact with your publisher other than receiving money from time to time - hopefully in large quantities! However, you may want to meet the publisher to discuss revisions, new editions and, hopefully the publication of your next book.

Publishing for e-readers

If you are using a publisher for a printed book, you might wish to create an e-book at the same time and your publisher will be able to do this for you at little extra cost since there are many common aspects in the publishing process. However, many writers only wish to self publish for the e-reader market and, in this section, we consider the possible benefits of engaging the services of a publisher when it is possible - indeed easy - to publish by yourself.

Services such as Kindle Direct Publishing provide a convenient and easy way of creating and distributing e-books, so why would an author approach a publisher for assistance and pay for the privilege?

One should not undervalue the services of a professional with respect to such aspects as proofreading, editing, layout, internal images, cover design (yes, you do need one!) and promotional material. Unfortunately, the e-book market is often criticised because of the poor quality of many publications. It is all too easy, not to mention tempting, to complete a book and upload it for publication without any proofreading or, equally importantly, some editing. Many writers believe that, because they are competent in spelling and grammar, they will not make mistakes and that any unintentional slips will be picked up by their word processor. Alas, this is sadly not the case and the author is the least likely person to spot their own errors. Also, one should not be so arrogant to believe that you have created the perfect script - an outsider can often provide an insight as to what the reader might expect as opposed to how the writer, in the glory of creation, might have presented. The self publishing author should, at least, involve others prior to publication but should consider the benefits of using professionals who might make all the difference between good and bad reviews and hence sales.

We have looked at the process of creating an e-book in chapter 3 and other issues are covered elsewhere in this book, so here we shall only draw attention to the differences between an e-book and its printed counterpart. For an e-book, formatting should be kept to an absolute minimum, pages should not be numbered, the typeface and point size should be chosen with regard to ease of reading and adjustability, and tables should be used with caution. Generally there will be no indexing other than a table of contents, a cover image is normally required, although no back cover is used. An ISBN is generally necessary although if you are only publishing with Amazon, they do have their own identification system. Legal Deposit requirements now cover e-books - see chapter 7 for further details. Set-up costs for e-books are obviously minimal, as are distribution costs which are generally borne by the buyer according to the size of the digital file. There is also the contentious issue of digital security which is not essential but may be required by some distributors.

A publisher can advise you on the above issues and also take care of the details for you. However, self publishing an e-book is straightforward and services such as Kindle Direct Publishing provide an easy route. Further details of KDP can be found in chapter 10 of this book.

6. PRICING GUIDANCE AND DISCOUNTS

Publishing for print on demand and e-readers enables the author to set the cover price and receive most of the profits. Whilst this approach may not have the benefits of the marketing and distribution facilities provided by traditional publishers, the returns per copy to the author can be significantly higher.

In this chapter, we consider different approaches to setting a realistic cover price in relation to an acceptable return per copy. Most of the discussion is based around print on demand physical books and assumes that you have an account with a mainstream POD printing company e.g. Lightning Source. Alternative options are mentioned in chapter 10.

Set Up Costs

Unless you are using one of the 'free' services such as CreateSpace, you will have to pay to set up your book with the POD company. The basic cost is in the region of £50 for the cover, interior, and annual catalogue fee. However, you should allow double this figure overall, to include a proof copy, ISBN and possible revision to cover or interior. You will also probably want to order some copies to give away or send for review and you will need at least one copy (two in the US) for legal deposit (see chapter 7). You might also want to provide some marketing and promotion for your book and this will entail some additional cost (see chapter 9).

Discounts Explained

For print on demand books, most sales are likely to be either on-line or through direct sales by the author. If the sales are on-line, the seller will naturally want a fee to cover their costs. Even if the books are supplied directly to the author at cost price, some financial incentive is useful for prospective buyers or for local agents stocking and selling the books.

It is suggested that the cover price is not printed on the book. This is not required and may prove unhelpful when using direct sales techniques or if a price change is made.

When setting the cover price, the author needs to allow a percentage of the cost that will be given to booksellers, whether they be on-line retailers, major booksellers, or local stockists. This percentage is known as the discount and can typically vary between 20% and 55% of the cover price. On-line retailers such as Amazon may accept a discount as low as 20% or 25% whereas main book stores might want 55% (or more). The standard discount rates are: retailer 40%, wholesaler 55%, and distributor 65% to 75%. See Shepard [5] for further explanation.

For books supplied direct to the author, the actual discount given to different sellers may vary according to what they are offering, but in setting the cover price, the author must consider the various sales options and set a cover price that will generate a sufficient return in any selected method. However, you will need to set the discount at the time of publication, so it is useful to consider such matters before beginning the process.

Working on the basis that most books will be sold on-line or direct selling by the author and local retailers, the discount could realistically be set at 25%. This need only apply to the on-line sales and there seems little reason to offer Amazon any more. For example, a 200 page hardback book with cover price £15 might have a print cost of £6. After discount of £3.75, the on-line sales would return £5.25 per copy to the author. Also, the author could order a direct supply of, say, 100 copies and sell directly to local buyers. In this case, the author might want to offer some advantage in buying direct as opposed to on-line and perhaps reduce the price to £12 per copy. The cost to the author, including postage, would amount to about £6.20 per copy giving a return of £5.80 per copy.

Alternatively, or in addition, the author could approach local retailers to stock and sell a few copies of the book. Here, decisions need to be made on the cover price and discount offered. One approach would be to revert to the standard cover price and discount; however, the retailer might be reluctant if the author was known to be selling directly at a reduced price. A compromise is suggested whereby the local retailer could offer the book at say, £12.99 per copy and receive a 25% discount of £3.25, giving a return of £3.54 per copy to the author. Not as good, but not that bad! However, the author should sell those copies to the retailer for an up-front fee on a non-returnable basis otherwise copies could be returned in a state that might be unfit for resale resulting in an overall loss.

Pricing

Bearing in mind the above discussion of discounts, the author needs to decide on a cover price that will yield a satisfactory return after discount and costs of print and supply. This can be calculated using a simple formula, as follows:

$$R = C(1\text{-}D) - P$$

Where:
R is the financial return per copy to the author
C is the cover price, set by the author
D is the discount expressed as a decimal
P is the print cost per copy (including delivery)

For example, if the cover price is £7.50, the discount is 40% (which we write as 0.4) and the print cost is £2.50 then:

Return per copy = £7.50 x 0.6 - £2.50 = £2

Obviously, the author would like a large return for each copy which, in turn, means a higher cover price making it less attractive to the buyer. On the other hand, the author could set a more attractive price but end up making a loss!

One approach to deciding the price is to start off by working out the break-even price where the returns are zero. Using the above equation and setting R=0, we get (after a little rearrangement):

C = P/(1-D) as the break-even cover price.

For example, using the above figures of a 40% discount and print cost of £2.50, then:

C = £2.50 / 0.6 = £4.17

So in this case, a cover price of £4.17 is the lowest price; anything higher will give the author a profit.

Probably the most sensible approach after establishing the minimum price is to look at other books of a similar genre, binding and interior and see what the going rate is. This should give a realistic idea of what the cover price should be, although it is worth asking a few friends for their reaction.

The beauty of using print on demand and selling on-line is that there are no issues of stocking, distribution and returns. However, if the author buys a consignment of books directly from the print on demand supplier, some of these issues may be relevant if using local retailers etc. to assist with direct sales. Stocking will not generally be a problem as the author need not order huge quantities although these will have to be paid for up-front. Similarly, distribution may not be an issue unless the author intends to sell direct to a wider audience where postage and packing need to be factored in to the overall price. Book returns should be avoided as far as possible.

Example Costs and Financial Returns

In this section, we consider the most popular methods of on-line and direct sales for which a lower discount rate (typically 25%) can be applied. The cover price of the book needs to be set prior to publication and this appears in the Nielsen book listings. This price is based upon the unit print cost, the discount, and the desired returns to the author, as described above.

Printing Costs

The print cost depends upon three factors: *colour or B&W interior, unit print price, price per page*. The unit cost depends upon the size of the book and the binding. With print on demand, the print cost is mostly influenced by the interior which can be colour or black and white.

Colour interiors are expensive and larger books with over 150 pages might not be viable. For example a 6 x 9 inch hardcover, colour interior with 200 pages would cost around £16 at current prices. This means that even with a short discount of 25%, the break-even price would be just over £21 which is significant in itself. However, a 100 page 8.5 x 5.5 inch colour paperback with similar discount would have a break-even price of around £5.60 which gives an opportunity to sell at an acceptable price and still make a profit.

Black and white interiors are most suitable for print on demand and can contain greyscale images. For comparison, a 6 x 9 inch hardcover, black and white interior with 200 pages would have a break-even cover price of £8 at a 25% discount and a 100 page 8.5 x 5.5 inch paperback would have a break-even price of only £3.31.

In recent times, another option has become available where some POD companies are offering colour inkjet printing. While the quality of images is not as good, the print costs are significantly lower and this may be a viable option for certain types of books. The per page print cost is about half that of premium colour printing and brings the unit cost down significantly for books with more than 100 pages.

Returns

As we have seen, the returns to the author per copy sold is:

Cover Price less Discount less Print Cost

In setting the cover price, we are trying to achieve a balance between a satisfactory return to the author and an acceptable price to the customer. A starting point for books with a black and white interior is to consider a cover price which is three times the print cost.

For the sake of example, let us use a cover price of three times the unit print price, rounded down to a convenient price.

A 200 page 8 x 5 inch paperback might have a print cost of around £2.70 so a cover price might be set at £7.95. With a 25% discount, the profit per copy would be £3.26.

A 200 page 6 x 9 inch hardcover would have a print cost around £6 with a cover price of £18. In this case the profit per copy would be £7.50. Perhaps a cover price of £15 might sound more attractive to prospective buyers, but even so the profit per copy would be £5.25 – still an acceptable return for the author!

As we have said, colour books have a higher print cost and only realistic for up to say 150 pages unless you can accept the cheaper inkjet option. Let us therefore give some examples based upon a 150 page book in premium colour.

The 8 x 5 inch paperback would cost around £5.95 to print and with a cover price of £17.95 would yield a return of £7.51. The author could afford to give a bigger discount or reduce the cover price to, say £14.95. At this price the return would be £5.26.

An 8.5 x 5.5 inch colour hardback with 150 pages would cost around £9.25 to print and even if we were to sell at £19.95, the return would be £5.71 per copy.

In the above examples, we have calculated the returns after setting the cover price. An alternative approach is to decide on the returns that we want and calculate the cover price. If we re-arrange the original pricing formula in the form used for our break-even analysis, we get:

$$C = (R + P)/(1-D)$$

So, in the above example for our colour hardback, if we approached this on the basis that we would be happy to receive £4 per copy (i.e. $R = 4$) and using $D = 0.25$ and $P = £9.25$, we get:

$$C = (4 + 9.25)/(1 - 0.25) = 13.25/0.75 = 17.67$$

In other words, the cover price would need to be £17.67 to give a return of £4.

On the other hand, if the inkjet colour printing was sufficient, the 150 page, 8.5 x 5.5 inch colour hardback would have a print cost of around £6.55 ($P=6.55$). If we wanted a return of £4 per copy ($R=4$), with a discount of 25% ($D=0.25$), then our Cover Price, C, is:

$$C = (4 + 6.55)/(1 - 0.25) = 10.55/0.75 = £14.07$$
$$\text{(round down to £14)}$$

If your book exceeds 150 pages and you need colour, then the cheaper inkjet option is probably the only viable one. Suppose that you wish to produce a 250 page, 8.5 x 5.5 inch, colour hardback with a £4 return per copy. If you choose premium colour the cover price would be £22.33, whereas the inkjet version would work out at £16.33 and that £6 difference could be the key to sufficient sales! However, if your book requires quality images and a heavier paper, don't sacrifice quality for profit - it won't do your reputation any good in the long run!

All the above prices are for guidance only and are based upon those applicable in 2014. You will need to check the details with your particular POD printer and take careful note of any addition costs, production and delivery times, and any other charges or commitments. Also, be aware that your book will usually be available worldwide and subject to financial and other regulations applying in those countries.

Apart from using the above calculations, it is important to repeat the earlier advice to compare your book to similar ones on the market and set the price accordingly.

Pricing for e-books

Setting the price for an e-book is very different to that of a printed book. This time, the main relevant factors are discount and required returns, but you may find yourself confined by the market and your chosen distributor. Generally, e-books have no setup costs and no real production costs, other than a small charge for download - typically 10p per megabyte (a typical e-book would be less than 5 megabytes). Many authors choose to use Kindle Direct Publishing (KDP) which is essentially a free service - further details and alternatives can be found in chapter 10.

Considering e-books in relation to KDP, there are some clear guidelines on their website, see: https://kdp.amazon.com/help?topicId=A37Z49E2DDQPP3 for initial guidance and links to further details. Amazon set limits on your pricing, depending on whether you select their 35% or 70% royalty options. It would generally be more sensible to select the 70% option if it is available in your country. The current guidance for the UK is that the cover price should be set between £1.49 and £7.81 and that the e-book should be priced at least 20% below a printed version.

So, in setting a cover price for your e-book, the situation is somewhat simpler - basically charge what you want between those limits, while matching it up to similar e-books! However, authors should be aware that VAT applies to e-books and that, from January 1st 2015, the VAT rate will change from the supplying country to the consuming country. This means that, in the UK, e-books will be subject to a 20% VAT charge. According to Amazon, 'the price limits of 1.49 and 7.81 GBP will remain and the element that will change will be the extra charge for the VAT depending of the country'.

The interpretation of this is that you can ignore tax rates in setting your price because the taxes will be applied to the consumer. However if Amazon applies 'price matching', the 'pricing' page of KDP states:

Royalty Rate x (Amazon price - taxes - Delivery Costs) = Royalty

So you should be prepared to take a 20% cut! Delivery costs are not likely to be high for a standard text-only book of typically 0.5MB, although a lot of images can significantly increase the size: a 'graphic guide' of 180 pages might be around 15MB (a delivery cost of £1.50)

7. OTHER PUBLISHING REQUIREMENTS

ISBNs and Barcodes

Every book should have an ISBN if it's going to be accessible by the general public. The ISBN (International Standard Book Number) is a number that uniquely identifies any given book.

Different editions and different formats of the same book require separate ISBNs. For example, a book that has been initially published as a hardback and subsequently as a paperback would need distinct ISBNs.

Books for e-readers will generally also need an ISBN if they are to be available to retailers. There are different formats of e-books and so if an e-book is released on more than one platform, each should have its own ISBN.

The ISBN used to be a 10-digit number but since 2007, it is 13 digits long and hyphenated to indicate such information as country of origin, publisher and title. Because part of the code identifies the publisher, a new ISBN should be obtained if the author transfers their book to a different publisher even if no changes have been made to the content or cover.

Amazon uses a form of the old ISBN that it calls the ASIN (Amazon Standard Identification Number) for its own identification purposes, although they still use the ISBN for external reference. Further details are given in [6].

In the UK, the allocation of ISBNs is governed by the Nielsen UK ISBN Agency. ISBNs are not available individually; they must be bought in blocks of at least 10. A publisher normally buys larger blocks of ISBNs and the unit cost is significantly lower. Further details for ISBNs in the UK can be found on Nielsen's website [10]. Details for ISBNs in the US can be found at [9] along with other general information.

The ISBN is usually accompanied by a barcode on the back cover of a book. This will be required if the book is distributed through retail outlets. The barcode can contain a 5 digit extension to identify the price of a book.

A barcode can be obtained commercially or produced by home software. You can also obtain a free barcode from some websites - an example is [11].

The barcode should be printed at the designated size and resolution. Some print on demand printers will automatically generate a barcode when a book is submitted.

The Structure of a Book

When the book has been written, there are still some items that require attention. These may include: title page, copyright page, dedication, acknowledgements, foreword, table of contents, table of illustrations, preface, introduction, index, bibliography, appendices, glossary, and footnotes. Your publisher may be able to help you with these, but be prepared to spend some time getting this right. This book can be used as an example of typical content and layout, but there are acceptable variations and the reader is advised to look at books in their genre for current practice and variations. Some general guidance is given below:

Title Page: this is usually the first printed page in the book and gives the title, sub-title, author, name of the foreword writer, the publisher, and publishing year. Sometimes the title page is preceded by an abbreviated form of the same page containing only the main title and followed by an additional page containing a picture or information such as other works by the same author.

Title Verso Page: alternatively, this might be called the copyright page. It appears on the reverse of the title page and typically contains information about the edition, the publisher, the ISBN, an assertion of copyright, and a statement regarding rights and permissions relating to copying and reproduction. The latter does not have to be totally prohibitive e.g. Shepard [5], [6] gives permission to copy or reprint portions for non-commercial use.

Dedication: this is usually a separate page containing a short statement dedicating the book to a person or persons in a brief sentence. A short, sensible and reasoned statement that can be appreciated by the reader is an appropriate form. A dedication that appears to be directed to the reader has some merit. The author is advised to look at various books to gauge an appropriate style.

Acknowledgements: this page is occasionally part of the dedication or title verso page but, more appropriately, it is a separate page that is usually associated with non-fiction books to acknowledge the contribution of people who have assisted in the production of the book with specialist knowledge, critical review, and otherwise unacknowledged contributions. This is best presented as a straight testimony with specific reference to individual contributions. Gushing praise to one's parents, friends and faith may make the author feel glorious but does little to inspire confidence in the substance of the publication.

Foreword: this is a short introduction written by an informed or noted person, other than the author, as a commendation of the book.

Table of Contents: often abbreviated to 'Contents' – this is essentially a list of chapter headings and associated page numbers. Non-fiction books will often have sub-headings within chapters and it is helpful to the reader to supply these sub-headings and their respective page numbers in the table of contents. Some fictional books may sub-divide chapters but it is unlikely to be of much practical use to include references to these in the table.

Table of Illustrations: this is relatively rare in modern books as the illustrations and/or photographs are set in context. However, if the author believes that the reader could usefully benefit from such an index, there is no reason not to include it.

Preface: this is usually written by the author and is used to describe the book and the background reasons for writing it. If no separate acknowledgement page is used, then this section can serve to thank those involved.

Introduction: this is the last section before the main body of work, although it may form the first chapter. It is perhaps more applicable to non-fiction books than fiction; in the latter case it might be usefully employed to provide some background information to the story. For non-fiction books, this can be used to introduce essential concepts or to summarise historical background.

Index: generally, this only applies to non-fiction books and despite being a tedious chore to compile, it provides a valuable resource to the reader when using the book as a reference source. To this end, when a topic is referred to in many different parts of the book it is helpful to indicate, in bold, the most relevant section(s). Accuracy in indexing is vital and is best left until the stage when all proofreading, corrections, and layout has been finalised.

Bibliography: again, applying mainly to non-fiction books where references are made to other pieces of work or where passages have been quoted, suitable acknowledgement should be made with a reference to the original work given in the bibliography. Standard formats exist and an example can be found at the end of this book.

Appendices: another feature of non-fiction books is a section at the end of the book containing an appendix or appendices. These might take the form of tables of technical data or explanatory information. Generally, these contain supplementary information that would otherwise obscure the message of the main text but could be of useful reference material to the reader.

Glossary of Terms: yet another category that mainly applies to non-fiction, although some fictional works might usefully include such a list. Often just called a *Glossary*, this is a list of technical terms with a definition for each. The main text may also define a term on its first appearance but such a list is still a very useful reference source for readers. An example can be found at the end of this book.

Footnotes: some publications make extensive use of footnotes within the main body of the text. These are usually superscripted numbered references on each page with corresponding text at the foot of the page or end of the chapter. They may be used to serve as a bibliography, mini-appendix, or short glossary. They can be useful in providing an 'instant' reference but there are obvious limitations. If a book is likely to be offered as an e-book, footnotes are best avoided as they are difficult to replicate in this format.

In the above, we have looked at the structure and contents of a book, particularly non-fiction, although there are no hard and fast rules and if the author feels strongly, there is no reason to be bound by such rules. A nice example of conventional structure and individual style can be found at the start of Humphrys [2]. For fiction, see also Wodehouse [7] or have a browse through your own bookshelf. It is surprising how we often fail to notice differences in style and presentation until we look for them and yet once we have an understanding of a standard format and acceptable variations, we can devise one of our own that best suits the work to be published.

Technical Considerations

There are many issues in the production of a book that the author might not be aware of nor want to. The publisher will usually have assisted the author by providing services such as proofreading, editing and guidance for the structural issues as discussed above. However, the publisher has a particular role in the selection of such factors as: paper weight, trim size, margins, bleed, page numbering, blank pages, page count requirements, typeface, formatting, and layout. Some insight is provided here for the benefit of authors and as guidance for self publishing:

Print Options: the following discussion refers to standard print books; there are separate issues relating to e-books and these are considered later in this chapter. For print on demand books (or standard litho) the main considerations fall into two categories: book options and page details. We discuss these separately in the following text:

Book options concern the physical aspects of the publication: choices involve the cover and the interior. The cover may be hardback or paperback. Hardback options include stamped cloth bindings, laminates and dust jackets – not all options are available for different choices. The interior is largely influenced by the choice of colour or black and white, paper options and trim size.

Page details include choice of font, margins, alignment, page numbering etc. While these may appear trivial to the technically aware author, there are considerations that might not be apparent to other authors that a publisher will have the knowledge and experience to resolve. Most programs enable the creation of a master page which is useful to ensure consistency throughout a publication e.g. for margins.

Careful selection of font and font size needs to be made for the main body text. These days most people use a word processor and will be aware of popular fonts. The size will generally be 10 to 12 points and the font should be easy on the eye. Many people use Times New Roman when word-processing, but this is not generally a favoured choice for the printed page of a book. Consider using a sans serif font for an easier visual appearance. Choices also need to be made for the font and size of chapter and section headings and should be consistently applied throughout the book. Inappropriate choices may lead to an unprofessional appearance of the book.

There are no fixed rules for margins although some consideration needs to be made for printing and binding. Usually, a margin of at least ½ inch (13mm) should be set all around the text.

There are some issues regarding text alignment that are worth considering. This is largely a matter of personal preference. Some books use left alignment although this can give a jagged appearance on the right hand side of the page. A popular choice, however, is to justify the text to use both left and right alignment where spaces are usually added to achieve the result. This tends to give a more pleasing appearance, although it can result in some lines with a small number of long words looking rather odd. An alternative is offered by some programs by automatically inserting hyphens as word breaks to achieve justification.

Page numbering would seem, on the face of it, a simple operation. However the numbering for a typical book would not start on the first printed page, might have a separate numbering system for the pages preceding the main body of text (e.g. roman numerals), and might not include numbers for blank pages at the end of the book. The numbering would usually cease before the final printed page as items such as an index would normally not be included. Professional software usually has features permitting various numbering options.

Other considerations for page details might include consideration of graphical material, style of chapter headings, positioning and style of page numbers, and running heads (headers for pages within each chapter). Further discussion of page details is provided by Rich [3].

Considerations for e-readers.

Whilst many of the publication processes apply to e-books as well as printed books, it is worth considering the factors where e-books demand different treatment. Software is available to automatically generate an e-book from files in standard formats e.g. .doc. However, the use of these is unlikely to produce a good result for all but the simplest documents.

Traditionally, e-books have been created after the printed version of a book, but we are now seeing the emergence of e-books in their own right. We therefore look at the considerations in creating an e-book and whether this should be the only format, an accompanying format, or not at all.

A starting point is the type of book and its intended audience. Certain books such as technical manuals or text books are probably unsuitable as e-books although modern students are becoming used to accessing information electronically. If the text contains tables or graphical information, these might be difficult to present successfully on an e-reader screen. As most e-readers are currently black and white, a text that relies on colour will have a limited market.

As we have already mentioned, footnotes represent a problem as an e-book has no fixed pages. Similarly, any form of indexing would have to rely on hyperlinks which might make multiple references difficult or cumbersome.

Another choice to be made is the e-reader format(s) to release. Most e-readers use the popular epub format although Amazon's Kindle has its own azw format and will read mobi files. PDF files are widely accepted although illegal copying might be an issue. If releasing the same e-book in different formats, each format will require a unique ISBN as will a printed book.

The body text in an e-book will use a default font and size, although the user can set their own styles for headings. Limited use of bold or italics is permitted within the text.

Title and Sub-Title

Choosing a title – does it have to be unique? Rich [3] recommends a short title length of no more than six words – important for visibility in bookstores or on-line listings. Fiction and non-fiction books might require slightly different approaches in choosing a title. Fiction books do not generally have a sub-title. It is probably best to finalise the title after completing the book - many changes are made between conception and publication! Try to find a title that will interest prospective readers and encourage them to look further.

Sub-titles – generally used for non-fiction. Rich [3] suggests that a non-fiction work can use a quirky title and then use the subtitle to define what the book is really about. Shepard [6], when looking at on-line sales, suggests implanting key words within the sub-title to increase visibility in search engines. The sub-title does not have to appear on the cover.

Cover Design

The design of the front cover, spine and back cover are discussed by Rich [3] and Shepard [6]. This is generally best left to professionals because, unfortunately, people do tend to judge a book by its cover and a sub-standard design can deter people from looking further. For books that are going to be marketed on-line via such markets as Amazon where the book image is small, it is important that the front cover is clear with an easily readable title.

Print on demand printers will generally supply a bespoke template for the cover – including the back cover and spine, after supplying them with the relevant printing options. Specialist software will generally be required in order to create the cover using the template and producing a file that can be submitted to the standards for printing.

Some attention needs to be applied to the cover as, what may be technically correct, does not always produce the best visual results. For example, the binding of a hardback book can give the impression that the left hand side of the cover is inset within the gutter region. This may necessitate a greater right-hand margin to achieve a visually centred appearance.

The book's spine should clearly show the title and author's name. Conventionally, the wording should read from top to bottom, except where the book is thick enough to display the wording horizontally. Some spines also display the publisher's name and logo. Usually the title is the most prominent item on the spine although if the author is famous then the name can be the dominant item.

The back cover generally contains some information about the book's contents and the author. Also appearing are the ISBN, the barcode and the publisher's name and logo. Price can be included although it is best avoided for POD. The back cover is a marketing tool for the book and should indicate the content, why the book was written, the target readership, and the author's credentials. It is also useful to include any positive reviews or endorsements.

Surprisingly, perhaps, there are covers for e-books. When creating an e-book, two covers are produced. One is for marketing purposes and this would appear with the on-line listing. The other is a cover picture that is included in the e-book. The marketing cover would typically be a colour image while the internal cover would usually be a greyscale image. Size and resolution of these are discussed in the next section. The Amazon Kindle Publishing Guidelines [1] give further details on the inclusion of a cover image.

Illustrations and Photos

Both printed books and e-books can contain illustrations and photographs. The originals need to be scanned and saved to file either by yourself or your publisher. The following discussion covers image types, scanning issues, file types, and the incorporation of images into the final document.

Digital Image Types- Greyscale

We often refer to black and white images when, in fact, these usually contain a range of shades of grey. A more accurate term is *monochrome* for such images. When we scan a monochrome image it is converted to an array of dots, or *pixels*, that each have a value associated with it between 0 and 255. This value represents the shade of grey where 0 is black and white is 255. The range 0-255 is commonly used because this represents the range of values that can be stored in one byte of computer memory. Because a byte consists of 8 binary digits, or bits, the digital image is referred to as an 8-bit greyscale image.

Digital Image Types- Colour

Colour images require a combination of three primary colours for each pixel. We are familiar with the so-called RGB model in which colours are obtained by mixing red, green and blue light in different proportions. These are called additive colours as the red, green and blue components are added to a black background. Storage requires 1 byte for each colour, hence we refer to a 24-bit colour image. Printers prefer another system based upon an alternative colour model – the CMY model which is a subtractive system based upon subtracting proportions of cyan, magenta and yellow from a white background. Printing with CMY inks does not give a good result for black and so a four-colour system is used based upon cyan, magenta, yellow and black (CMYK). When creating a book, colours can be set to the CMYK space at the stage of creating the final PDF document. For black on the cover, it is recommended to use 'rich black', where the CMYK proportions are 60:40:40:100.

Scanning

Scanning software enables the user to select various options. One of these will be the document type and will typically offer a selection from colour, grey, or black and white and these are self explanatory. Other options are usually scan size, output type, and resolution. The scan size enables smaller sizes to be selected to speed up scanning. Output type offers a choice between black and white, greyscale, or colour. Resolution refers to the number of dots per inch (dpi) and this determines the quality of the scanned result. A resolution of 100 dpi means that each square inch of the original document is translated into a 100 x 100 grid of pixels. A higher resolution gives a better quality image but results in a bigger image file. Most print on demand printers set a maximum resolution of 300 dpi for both greyscale and colour images.

When the document has been scanned, the user will be invited to save the file and a variety of file formats are usually available. Some of these formats use compression to reduce the file size. Compression methods such as that used in jpeg involve a loss of detail and if the scanning resolution is only 300 dpi, this could lead to unsatisfactory results. Fortunately, there are ways round this. Usually, when creating a jpeg file, the user can select the level of compression or, inversely, the quality of the image. Choose highest quality (or lowest compression) for the best results. Another option if using jpeg, is to scan at a higher resolution – it means that the picture in your final document will be 'downsized' for the final printed file. Alternatively, just save the file in another format – for example the pcx format offers a so-called lossless compression so that you can save storage space without compromising image quality. It is worth checking that the publishing software can import the chosen file type.

A scanned image is not always perfect or perhaps the original was flawed, however there are ways to retrieve the situation. Typical problems involve marks and patterns, both of which can be resolved with some photo editing software. It is worth investing in some quality software to ensure that the final printed results are as good as possible. When including images, the publisher needs to consider problems of possible 'show through' where the lines of text on the reverse of the image page appear as faint stripes in the image. One solution is to put blank pages on the reverse of pictures or to arrange the pictures in a separate section. Alternatively, use a heavier paper if this is available.

Images for e-books

Basically, the same rules apply for e-books. Most images will be at 300 dpi, but the final form for the e-book is derived from a collection of files and images in a similar way to a web site. For Amazon Kindle, the preferred format for the marketing cover is a jpeg image of 600 x 800 pixels. Internal images will normally be jpeg at 300 dpi, although the same 'downsizing' rules applies for images submitted at a higher resolution. As most e-readers are monochrome, pictures and illustrations should be 8-bit greyscale images. Tables and certain lists are best presented as images to avoid problems with font size options available to the reader.

Legal Deposit Libraries

Legal Deposit libraries exist to collect and preserve published material so that it can be accessed by readers of today and future generations. In the UK, the Legal Deposit Libraries Act 2003 and Copyright and Related Rights Act 2000 set out the rules of governance for legal deposit.

There are six UK legal deposit libraries: These are the British Library, the National Library of Scotland, the National Library of Wales, the Bodleian Library Oxford, the Library of Cambridge University and the Library of Trinity College Dublin.

The British Library is entitled to receive a copy of any newly published book, without needing to request it. The publisher should therefore submit a copy of a new book to the British Library as a matter of course.

The other 5 legal deposit libraries are represented by the Agency for the Legal Deposit Libraries and it can request free copies of any material published in the United Kingdom and

Republic of Ireland to be sent directly to each of these libraries within twelve months of its publication.

Since April 2013, e-books are also included in the legal deposit requirements although, at the time of writing, the British Library is not yet ready to process digital content. Their website currently states 'If your electronic content requires a password, subscription or payment, the British Library or another legal deposit library will contact you as soon as we are ready to begin processing your material'. See www.bl.uk for the latest information.

Publication Date

When registering an ISBN, amongst other required information is the publication date. For self publishing authors and print on demand, this is not too critical. However, a realistic date of the first availability is useful because this date is supplied to all Nielsen's customers along with essential details of the book ahead of the publication date. This date is technically when the book goes to press and this may be different from when it is available to the public. The best approach is to set a publication date when it will actually be available to the public. If using print on demand, allow sufficient time for any corrections to be submitted and processed.

8. LEGAL ISSUES

This chapter is intended as an outline of the key legal issues that face writers and publishers. However, this is a complex area of the law and the details given are only the author's understanding of it. No liability is accepted for any loss or damage incurred as a result of following the text or information given here. The reader is advised to consult a qualified specialist lawyer in the event of any dispute or uncertainty.

The following discussion is based upon UK law but essentially applies to the US and most other countries that have ratified the terms of the Berne Convention, Universal Copyright Convention, or related international treaties.

Copyright

Copyright places restrictions on what other people can do with your work or their ability to make financial gain from it. It is a form of intellectual property right in a similar way to a patent or trademark. By establishing copyright, the author has some protection against plagiarism, unauthorised reproduction, adaptation and performance, including broadcasting.

Copyright is automatically established when a work is created and stored in some physical medium e.g. paper or computer disk. This is not restricted to completed works and applies to sections as they are created and recorded. Copyright can only be claimed for a work when some 'skill, judgement and labour' has gone into its creation, although this is reasonably easy to establish. Whilst this automatic copyright is legally sufficient, there may be practical reasons to go a little further.

In the previous chapter, we mentioned the copyright page (the title verso page) where a statement of copyright is usually made using the © symbol e.g. Copyright © 2014 Takahe Publishing Ltd. and this will be followed by some statement about restrictions and permissions regarding copying etc. Examples are easily found. The use of the © symbol is not essential, but a copyright statement may serve to deter plagiarism.

Some people advocate the use of the so-called *Poor Man's Copyright* whereby the author sends themselves a sealed, post dated package containing a copy of their work. This doesn't significantly add to the legal protection and is probably not worthwhile.

There is no particular need to seek special copyright arrangements covering the work in other countries. There are international agreements, including the important 1886 Berne Convention that was later enshrined in UK legislation by the Copyright, Designs and Patents Act of 1988. Also the Universal Copyright Convention was introduced in 1952 with less stringent conditions. The basic provisions of the Berne Convention and Universal Copyright Convention apply to most nations.

Copyright applies to a variety of works including books, plays, poems, drawings and photographs. Similarly computer software is also covered by copyright. It does not, however, apply to ideas – although this is a complex area. Basically, the idea itself is not copyright although a particular form or implementation is. For authors, this means that if you have an idea for a book and mention it to someone else before you make progress on paper, you are unlikely to have much legal recourse if the other person produces a book based upon the same idea.

There are some exceptions to the rules preventing copying and reproducing work from copyrighted sources. These are generally relevant to non-fiction works. In the UK and some other countries there is a concept of *fair dealing* in which it is legally acceptable to copy certain copyrighted material. This includes copying for research purposes, reporting and professional advice. There are guidelines for the amount of material that can be used and these are readily available online. Providing copyrighted material in an adapted form for visually impaired people is also permitted without the need for permission.

In other respects, it is also possible to quote small sections from other sources as long as due acknowledgement is given. Extensive quotations from one source are not usually acceptable, particularly if writing a book that could be seen as competing with the source. Phrases that are known to be common knowledge do not need acknowledgement. With all quotations, great care should be taken to ensure that these are accurate in every respect.

Lists and tables from other publications are also copyrighted and care should be taken in reproducing them. The author should, at least adopt their own format and use selected content rather than just replicate the original material. Again, acknowledgement of the source should be given and, If in any doubt, seek permission!

When choosing a title for a book, there is no essential requirement for uniqueness as long as one is not intending to pass it off as the original. However, most fiction authors would seek an original title for their work and a simple on-line search should prevent accidental duplication. For non-fiction, duplicate titles are commonplace e.g. Engineering Mathematics. There is no harm in this and may even have some benefits in assisting students to find a suitable work within a specific area. Many such books also use sub-titles that may provide uniqueness and help to identify the approach taken by the author or the academic level of the intended audience.

It is up to the copyright holder to detect any infringements of copyright and to enforce their rights – usually at their own expense. For small scale infringements it may not be worthwhile to pursue an action through the civil courts. Nevertheless, the author or publisher should not let these activities go unnoticed and should at least send a warning letter to the offender with a threat of legal action. There is, at least, the possibility of an out-of-court settlement. However, infringement of copyright for a major book is a serious matter that might represent a significant loss of income for the owner. Remedies include damages, an injunction, or destruction of published materials.

Copyright used to exist for fifty years after the author's death and this was a rule established under the Berne Convention and applied to most countries. Under The Duration of Copyright and Rights in Performances Regulations Act 1995, copyright in the UK now lasts until seventy years from the end of the calendar year of the author's death and the changes applied retrospectively. This harmonised the regulations in EU countries and the situation is similar in the US and many other parts of the world. Variations may apply to works other than of a literary nature. The reader is referred to Circular 15A from the US Copyright Office [21] for an indication of the complexity of copyright law. Another interesting example is the recent court action in the US between Arthur Conan Doyle's estate and Leslie Klinger, see http://guardianlv.com/2014/06/sherlock-holmes-ruled-public-domain/ for details.

Copyright is identified in the assertion of so-called *economic* rights. In addition, there are *moral rights* for the protection of the reputation of the author. These include the right to be identified as the author (*paternity right)*, the right to object to derogatory treatment (*integrity right*), and the right not to be falsely attributed as the author of a work. The first of these means that the author has the right to be properly credited for the work and essentially applies to when the work has been adapted for a play, TV or film. The second of these covers adaptations that severely distort the original work or malign the reputation of the author. The right regarding *false attribution* protects the author against being wrongly identified with other works that might benefit from the author's reputation or that might be detrimental to the reputation.

Copyright can be assigned by the owner to another party on a temporary or permanent basis. This is particularly important in the dealings between an author and a publisher and we refer to a *temporary grant of licence.*

Publishing Contracts

Any author using the services of a publisher will be required to sign a contract and this should be read carefully beforehand. The author must understand exactly what the contract commits them to and avoid signing away rights or entering into excessively binding contracts. Similarly, it should be understood what the publisher is committing to. The following discussion outlines some of the issues that would typically be covered in a contract between an author and a publisher offering assisted self publishing services.

The author will usually agree to supply the manuscript in an agreed format and within some agreed time scale. If the manuscript is hand written and requires transcription then the publisher might require specific payment for this service. The contract will usually specify all fees and how these are to be paid. There should be some agreed timetable and details for activities involving both the author and the publisher so that the book can be produced, checked, and made available in time for a mutually agreed publication date.

During the publishing process, changes to the manuscript might be required by the author or the publisher. The contract should be clear about what is allowed in this respect, when such changes can be made, and if any fees will be charged. The publisher will probably assert their right to remove content that might be contentious or even to withdraw their services if the material is generally unacceptable. In any event, the contract should cover such eventualities and provide a facility for dispute resolution. Changes will also arise through editing and proofreading. The author should be clear as to what the publisher is offering in this respect and to what extent they have control over any amendments.

The publisher will establish copyright for the edition of the manuscript that it publishes and this copyright will remain throughout the duration of the contract. However, ownership of the material is that of the author and, on termination of the contract, the publisher should relinquish all further rights to the material. This should be specified in the contract along with provision for revisions and new editions. Consideration should be given to the duration of the contract and how it might be terminated by either side and, in that case, what will happen e.g. with copies yet to be sold, existing print on demand arrangements, related payments and return of electronic files to the author.

The contract should also clearly identify the level of remuneration to the author and how often and by what means such payments should be made. This may depend upon the volume of sales and payments to the author may be less frequent if sales are very small.

The publisher should make clear undertakings such as ISBN allocation and legal deposit copies; these should be considered a necessary provision. For self publishing, assisted self publishing services will generally not commit to advertising and promotion, although they may offer some guidance. Any offerings in this respect should be considered non-existent unless specified in the publishing contract.

Miscellaneous Issues

We have already mentioned that, in the UK, there is a legal requirement to submit one copy of a published book to the British Library within one month of publication. From April 2013 this requirement extended to e-books and other electronic publications. This process is known as 'legal deposit' and further details relevant to the UK can be found in chapter 7 of this book. There are similar requirements in the US, where two copies need to be sent to the United States Copyright Office for the use of the Library of Congress. Similar laws apply in most other countries and this raises a potential problem with regard to international distribution and the legal deposit requirements of different countries. For example, according to the US Copyright Office: 'If you distribute your work in the United States, you are subject to the deposit requirements of the United States. These requirements apply to a work that is first published in a foreign country as soon as that work is distributed in the United States through the distribution of copies that are either imported or are part of an American edition. The deposit requirement is one copy'. For the self publishing author, their books are generally listed on the various international sites of Amazon and it could be construed that copies bought on-line are imported and distributed. However, the British Library have told me that 'You are only legally bound if you are distributing your book in other countries. By selling your book through Amazon you are not bound to the legal deposit legislation of other countries'.

Individual authors and, by association, publishers must be very careful to avoid accusations of libel and costly legal actions. Libel is a form of defamation and involves the *publication* of *false* information about someone to their **detriment** and is a matter for the civil courts. For non-fiction works, an author can ensure that reference to living characters is true, fair and balanced. If the characters in question are deceased, it is generally held that they cannot be defamed since they cannot be subject to personal detriment. However a recent European Court ruling, as reported in the Law Society Gazette stated: 'It accepted that the reputation of a deceased family member might affect a person's private life and identity if there was a sufficiently close link between the person affected and the reputation of his or her family, thus bringing actions within the scope of Article 8 of the European Convention on Human Rights'. With regard to living characters, authors must ensure that any direct references can be robustly defended in terms of the generally accepted forms of defence: truth or fair comment. The author of fiction could inadvertently stray into libellous material through association to actual living people and it is common to insert a statement at the start of the book such as: 'All characters in this book are entirely imaginary and any resemblance to any living individual is entirely coincidental'. However, such a statement is unlikely to withstand a legal challenge and the author should make some basic checks prior to publication. In the internet age, it is easy to conduct searches on names of people and any potential conflicts should be readily avoided by suitable changes to the manuscript.

The other main legal issue for an author is that of plagiarism and consequent actions under copyright law. While some of these issues have been considered in the early parts of this chapter, some of the less obvious pitfalls are mentioned here. In works of fiction there may well be disputes over originality even though no intentional plagiarism has occurred. We have seen that an idea, in itself does not form copyright until some practical implementation is made. Thus, coincidence or similarity in some themes might genuinely occur and it would take detailed examination to conclude that some copying had taken place. It is also recognised that an element of 'sub-conscious copying' can occur when one has read works many years earlier and some aspects of these are inadvertently reproduced. This is a complicated area and it could be argued that, given the total amount of fiction produced over the years, it would be nearly impossible to not produce themes existing in other works. The situation regarding non-fiction is perhaps more straightforward. It is common for different books to cover the same subject material although individual authors will try to present the material with a particular style and different content. Textbooks for students are a classic example - particularly in the sciences where the books generally cover the same topics and the fundamental theories do not vary. However, in the broader context of academic texts, it is necessary to draw upon other studies and there are rules governing paraphrasing, citation and attribution - guidance can be found on almost any university website.

9. MARKETING AND PROMOTION

With self publishing using print on demand, you do not get the level of marketing and promotion offered by most traditional publishers. If you opt for assisted self publishing, your publisher may offer a small amount of support, but essentially it is up to you to promote your book.

If you are expecting your new novel to be a blockbuster success with millions of sales worldwide, then perhaps self publishing is not the right method for you - although some self published Kindle books have had great success.

Many self publishing authors produce non-fiction books with a limited target audience, where the use of print on demand is most applicable. In many cases, the author will order a consignment of their own books and sell these directly through local sources. This type of book will not be attractive to major litho-based publishers as returns would likely not even cover the cost of printing, let alone distribution and marketing costs.

However, the author can make a reasonable profit by publishing in this way and, as the book will be available through Amazon and listed with other booksellers, there is a reasonable prospect of selling additional copies on-line.

Marketing Provided by a POD Publisher

Using the services and resources associated with assisted self publishing is an attractive option for many authors and, although there is not usually the level of marketing and promotion that you would associate with a traditional publisher, you might expect to be provided with one or more of the following:

Amazon: For sales of books over the internet, Amazon is the dominant on-line retailer with a worldwide marketplace and excellent marketing strategies. Most POD book publishing includes a listing on Amazon and the author is not involved in the supply and delivery costs of books ordered through this source. There is an option for creating a *Look Inside* facility within the Amazon listing which can help to boost sales. The publisher may also offer to provide a Kindle option for a small extra fee.

Nielsen: When your publisher assigns an ISBN to a book, additional information about the book is provided to Nielsen who administer ISBNs in the UK. This information is distributed to major booksellers worldwide and provides a means for the book to be ordered from any of these stores. Nielsen's customers include Amazon.co.uk, Waterstones, WH Smith, Gardners, Betrams, Askews Library Services, Play.com, and Blackwells.

Espresso Book Machine: In chapter 3, we described a machine that could provide an instant POD capability within bookstores. This facility may become more widespread, particularly as the high street bookshop comes under pressure from internet marketing. Many POD books are eligible for Espresso availability and this is an option that could be worth consideration.

Publisher's Website: Some publishers operate a sales section on their website that features books published by them and allows members of the public to purchase copies. However, the author should check that this is not the only on-line availability and they should also check what returns are offered from on-line sales as well as the cost of direct supply.

Dedicated Website: Some publishers will create a dedicated webpage for your book with links direct to its Amazon listing as part of their publishing package. It is useful if the author is encouraged to be involved in the design and choice of content for this web page and can provide information about local availability and links to other relevant sites. There are also possibilities to establish links from other websites to the book's web page.

Promotion Guidance for Authors

There are also many things that an author can do to promote their book. You may find that your publisher can also advise or provide help in some of these respects. A few suggestions are outlined below.

Book Reviews: Send out copies of your book to relevant literary reviewers prior to the publication date, if possible. Check first that the reviewer is interested. Include a comprehensive press release (see below). Send the book in galley form if necessary.

Book Promotion Events: If you have a local bookseller, it could be worth checking if they would host a book signing event. They might be a little reluctant in the case of a POD book but perhaps sympathetic to a local author. You will have to do a deal with regard to them stocking some copies and this will inevitably raise the question of discount and returns, but if it helps to promote the book then it's worth a try.

Alternatively, you could arrange your own event. First you will need to find a venue - preferably indoors. This might be a local theatre, church hall, school, library, etc. Be prepared to give a short talk about your book with, perhaps, some readings from it accompanied by some visual aids. You will need to have sufficient copies of your book to sell at the event - preferably at a discounted price.

Any book promotion event will require a lot of planning and double checking that all arrangements are in place. Above all, you will need an audience and your advertising will need to be sorted out well in advance. Inform local press and radio by sending them details - try and get these in a form that they can use directly e.g. write a short article in the style that your local paper might use for a forthcoming event or how an announcement might be made over local radio.

When the day comes, allow enough time to deal with any problems. Check beforehand with other people involved that they are ready, know what they have to do, when they have to do it, and what they have to bring along. Allow for bad weather and make arrangements as necessary e.g. if the event is outdoors, what will you do if it is raining? If you are indoors and the weather is cold, can you turn the heating on? Do the lights work or do any bulbs need replacing? Arrive early and get set up in good time. If you are using a microphone, check that it works, check sound levels and make sure that you don't start off with ear-piercing feedback!

Try and fix a starting time for your event but don't make this the same time as your talk - people won't arrive on the dot, so allow some margin for people to gather and have something for them to do e.g. have a coffee and browse some exhibits for ten to fifteen minutes. But the start time of your talk should be clear - you don't want people to wander off thinking that they've seen everything before you start talking!

Keep your talk short and interesting. Make sure that you have rehearsed it and try to make it as natural as possible. Keep it light hearted and try to engage the audience. Don't get carried away with the sales pitch but try to interest them sufficiently that they will want to buy your book and find out more. And, of course, offer to sign any copies that they buy.

Local Advertising

It is tempting to think that by taking out an advert in your local paper or by getting a leaflet printed and distributing it door to door might be an excellent way of telling the world about your new book and thereby generating lots of sales. Don't bother! Save your money! Most advertising is a complete waste of time and money! What do you do with those glossy pizza adverts that come through your letter box every day? How much time do you spend looking at the adverts in your local paper - the chances are you don't even notice half of them! That's not to say that all advertising is not worthwhile - you just have to be pragmatic in your thinking and decision making, unless you just happen to have lots of money to throw around!

One of the best forms of advertising is free advertising! If you can get a small article published in your local newspaper about your new book, you have not only got a free advert but people are more likely to read it. You can send out the details of your book to local papers and radio in the form of a *Press Release*. This would typically be a single-page document of about 500 words and follows some basic conventions with regard to style and layout with the aim of getting people interested in your new book. There is plenty of information and guidance freely available on the internet regarding press releases and the reader is also referred to Rich [3] for further details and other publicity advice.

The press release should be written in an informative 'news' style, avoiding an advertising pitch. Keep sentences reasonably short and use about four or five to the paragraph. The most important information should be in the first two paragraphs as many people do not read beyond this! The exact layout can vary slightly, but should be along the following lines:

Header: 'Press Release' and release timing detail e.g. 'FOR IMMEDIATE RELEASE'
Contact Details - name, telephone, e-mail
Title and Sub-Title

Body: First paragraph starts with location and date then include the essential: who, what, where, when, why and how components

Further paragraph(s): more about the book, target audience, availability etc.

Final paragraph about the author, contact details, website etc.

Footer: # # # (standard finish to indicate there is no more material)

Note that in the above, we are assuming the press release originates from someone other than the author e.g. the publisher and hence the contact details will differ. The release will carry greater weight if it comes from someone other than the author and preferably in some professional capacity.

The press release can be sent by e-mail and included in the body of the e-mail. Remember that journalists are busy people and will want to access your message quickly and easily. If you send your release as an attachment, send it as a text file or as a Word document (save it as the older .doc format just in case they don't have an up to date version of Word!). To find out who to send it to, look at the 'Contact Us' section of the website for your selected media. There may be a specific reference for press releases, otherwise you may be able to identify the correct channel from a list of relevant people. If you're totally stuck, telephone the offices and ask who you should send it to.

Promotional Materials

Another form of advertising is in the form of posters, bookmarks, postcards etc. This will usually cost you some money, so only invest in what you think may bring about some sales.

A poster might be one that you use to directly advertise your book and you might find friendly places who will display it for free. To this end, you might stand more chance if it doesn't take up too much valuable space, so an A5 poster may be quite acceptable. Also, keep the poster looking its best by getting it laminated it won't cost much and will give a better impression.

Another type of poster is the 'cult' type which fans and enthusiasts might buy and display in their own homes. This is perhaps one associated with a type of novel - perhaps less so for 'The History of the Fishing Rod' - although you never know!

Bookmarks can be cheap to produce - try laminating a set of printed bookmarks and then guillotine to size. There might not be much merit in giving them to people who have already bought your book, so you need to think about how to distribute them to the best effect. The bookmark needs to be attractive and contain a simple advertising message about your book and how to get a copy.

Postcards are another possibility and are relatively cheap to produce - although if you are posting them to friends the cost of a stamp might make this an expensive form of advertising! You might be able to create a picture postcard for a place with your advertising message carefully included, but production costs may make this infeasible.

You could also produce small pads of themed notepaper with a subtle advertising message for your book. Other products could include drinking mugs, ballpoint pens, sticky tabs and so on. These are just ideas and you might find it fun to try one, but don't spend a lot of money - it is not likely to generate huge returns!

Local Distributors

You can usually sell your book through local retailers. They don't have to be bookshops - they could include the local hardware store, newspaper shop, post office, hairdresser, etc. The fact that you are a local author might be enough in itself and if your book is of relevance to the local community, so much the better.

You can't expect them to stock your book for nothing though. You will have to give them a discount on the cover price and that, in itself, might result in a price lower than that which customers would pay on-line. At first sight that might seem a bit counter intuitive - one expects the on-line price to usually be the cheapest. But think how it works. We have already said that if you are selling on Amazon, you might as well set the discount as low as you can e.g. 25%. Suppose your book has a cover price of £15, then Amazon will sell it at £15 and make £3.75 for themselves on each sale. If you buy direct from the POD printer, you can obtain your copies at cost, say £6 per copy. You could then let your local retailer sell them for £12 per copy and offer them a 25% discount. You supply the books to them at £9 per copy, they make £3 profit on each sale and you make the same. Your returns per copy are lower, but still more than you would usually get from a traditional publisher.

Normally, booksellers would want about 40% discount, but you might find local retailers more obliging. Your margins are still not great so you won't be able to allow returns of unsold copies. You will probably sell fewer books than you would through using a traditional publisher, so you need the higher financial returns per copy if the venture is going to be worthwhile.

One other thing - you need to prepare a small poster for each retailer to advertise your book. It needs to be the sort of thing that can be displayed conveniently in the window or inside the shop and should emphasise the local connection. You might want to leave the price blank to give the retailer some flexibility but whatever the price, it should be displayed by someone.

Social Media

In our modern times, we have the enormous power of social media e.g. Facebook, Twitter, LinkedLn, Google+, YouTube and Blogs to tell a large number of people about a new book and how they can get a copy. For example, you could create a Facebook page for your book and invite 'likes' from all your contacts. This is also another way of publicising events concerned with your book, to inform your fans about forthcoming publications and to get people discussing your current one. Do an internet search for Social Media Marketing for further advice and ideas.

Other Free Advertising

What about your workplace or that of your friends? Some companies have a local intranet on which staff can place adverts. Talk to your friends about advertising - they may have new ideas or contacts that you can use. Keep a lookout for places where you get a small poster put up. Your local pub or club might be able to help. Also local websites e.g. parish council may give you a free listing.

Groups and Societies with Similar Interests

Depending on the nature of your book, you might be able to find clubs and societies with similar or related interests. This will mostly be relevant to non-fiction books. Contact the group and make your work known to them. If they have a website, see if you can get a mention or a link. In return, you could link to them from your own website and perhaps even send them a free copy of your book.

Some Final Thoughts

The above list of ideas is not exhaustive and I'm sure that you can come up with a few ideas of your own. In your everyday life keep on looking for opportunities to plug your book and remember that if you are going to spend any money on advertising, make sure that it offers value for money. Also, don't forget that the best form of advertising is word of mouth so do your best to spread the word! Enlist the help of your friends and work colleagues and, if you are using a publisher, check to see if they can provide any free help - even if it's only the press release. But, returning to a previous topic, think carefully when setting the price for your book - with the best advertising in the world, if it's too expensive people won't buy it!

10. SELF PUBLISHING AND AMAZON

Background

Amazon is a huge on-line marketplace that offers an excellent way to sell your book or e-book on a worldwide basis. Founded in Washington USA in 1994, Amazon is essentially an American company and its main site is amazon.com which is the site used by residents of the US. The company also operates European sites for the UK (amazon.co.uk), Germany (amazon.de), France (amazon.fr), Spain (amazon.es) and Italy (amazon.it). In addition there are other sites for Canada (amazon.ca), Brazil (amazon.co.br), China (amazon.cn) and Japan (amazon.co.jp).

Although Amazon sells a wide range of goods, it is perhaps best known for its book sales - both new and second hand. The buying process is easy and it is often possible to have a glance inside before you buy. Delivery is as quick as you want it or usually free if you are prepared to wait a few days. E-books are available for the Kindle only, but again the process is simple and quick.

An author would be unwise to ignore the vast potential of Amazon in the sales of their book. Very often, a book will get automatically listed on Amazon when it is published. In this chapter, we look at how books get listed or the means by which authors and publishers can use Amazon to sell their book or e-book. Their website enables you to see how well your book is selling in relation to similar books. The reader is referred to Shepard [6] for a wealth of information about publishing for the Amazon marketplace.

Amazon's Own Print on Demand Service

Amazon runs its own POD service called CreateSpace. This was formed from two companies acquired by Amazon in 2005 - the original POD service for books was BookSurge founded in 2000. BookSurge and CreateSpace operated under their own names until 2009 when they were merged. Until recently it was not particularly attractive to UK authors because its operations were based in the US and the cost and delay of shipping to the UK were seen as off-putting. However, in May 2012, Amazon announced the launch of a European branch of CreateSpace and this now offers a viable option for UK authors. Note that, at the time of writing, European distribution is an option that you have to select from your account. The main website is still createspace.com and with a little searching you can find tables of shipping charges and times to the UK and other countries.

CreateSpace is an internet based POD publishing service. It allows authors to upload their manuscript in PDF or Word format and publish their book for free - although it's worth paying for a physical proof copy. This works in the same way as supplying books direct to the author which CreateSpace calls 'Member Orders' and books are supplied for the cost of printing and shipping from the US. Only softback covers are available, but low print costs theoretically make this an attractive option for authors who self-distribute their books, however at the time of writing it seems that shipping costs to the UK are still high. Using the CS online calculator in April 2014, 10 books would cost nearly £11 in shipping to the UK. Online sales involve a 40% retail discount whereas lower rates, down to 25%, can be set if you use Lightning Source. Books can be available to the general public through Amazon.co.uk and as these copies are printed in the UK, fast delivery options are available.

On-line, free publishing is obviously an attractive option for self publishing authors, although the process is still somewhat involved and choices may be restricted. The main competitors to CreateSpace offering low-cost internet publishing are Blurb and Lulu.

Blurb, based in San Francisco, California, was founded in 2004 and has websites in the US, North and South America and Europe, including Blurb.co.uk. However, books ordered for delivery in the UK are printed in the Netherlands and subject to a shipping charge which could be about £5 for a single book with the longest delivery time of about two weeks. As with CreateSpace, authors can upload their files and publish for free and Blurb offers downloadable software to assist. Blurb has an on-line bookstore that enables customers to preview and order books created on Blurb. The bookstore also features an author's bookshop for easy reference to other titles by the same author. Blurb now have an option to sell through Amazon but this might not always be very profitable once you have allowed for Blurb's supply cost and the margin required by Amazon. Authors can make their e-books available to the Apple iBookstore in addition to the Blurb bookstore.

Lulu was founded in 2002 and is based in Raleigh, North Carolina, but has six versions of its website for European customers including the UK (lulu.com/gb/en). They offer a free publishing service and authors can upload their manuscripts in Word or PDF format and use Lulu's online book creation software. A variety of book formats are available and authors keep 80% of the profits they set. Lulu offer a free ISBN or authors can supply their own. The company has its own bookstore, Lulu Marketplace, where registered customers can buy books. In addition, books can be made available on Amazon and other online retailers although these may incur price mark-ups. For distribution outside the Lulu Marketplace, authors must buy and approve a proof copy.

In comparison, CreateSpace comes out quite well in the field of online publishing resources. Whilst all of the above offer free setup, the use of book creation software, and optional fee-based support resources, CreateSpace automatically includes the Amazon marketplace and offers reasonable pricing and turnaround times. Some people have reported difficulties in getting assistance from CreateSpace when they have had problems, but generally the feedback from users is good.

Web based free publishing services like to give the impression that producing a book is easy but, in reality, there are many difficulties that may be encountered. If you are going to use one of these services, take the time to find out as much as you can beforehand, read the FAQs and user blogs - it could save you time and headaches in the long run!

Other Print on Demand Books

POD printers such as Lightning Source automatically list your book on Amazon, so the process is really very simple. Although the standard discount is 55%, the author can set a discount as low as 25% (with LSUK). A low discount may deter retailers from stocking or even handling a book but if most books are going to be sold through Amazon, there seems little point in setting a higher discount! The publisher determines the discount when they set up the book with the POD service. At the same time there is a requirement to say whether returns are permitted and the general advice here is not to allow returns if you are not hoping for the books to be stocked at normal retailers.

If you are intending to sell on Amazon, there are a few issues that are worth considering in relation to how this will appear on Amazon's website. Perhaps the best way to look at this is to consider things from the point of view of a prospective customer who will be unaware of your work and probably will not know much about the alternatives. This customer will typically start with a search by typing a short phrase e.g. 'Psychology for beginners'. The first thing you notice is that, as you type your search phrase a list of suggestions appears, based upon the words already entered. The search will bring up a list of books related to your search phrase with an emphasis on those books whose titles most strongly relate to key words in the search phrase. It should also relate to sub-titles where an author can attempt to include words that may be picked up by the search engine. Many authors have a title in mind before they start writing a book, but it is worth reconsidering this if you are intending to sell on-line. You will want your book to be prominent in any searches, so try to make the title include one or two key words, but avoid long titles. Shepard [6] discusses these issues in some depth and advocates rather lengthy sub-titles with inclusive key phrases, but these have a rather 'commercial' appearance and would not sit well with a UK readership for serious non-fiction books. There is perhaps much to be gained by taking the theme of your book, doing a few related searches on Amazon and be guided by the titles that come up. At the same time you can look at competing books with a view to setting a realistic cover price. Similarly, look at the cover pictures of the available books and see which ones stand out - use these observations as a guide towards your own cover design.

Books Created by Other Printers

As an alternative to print on demand, you may have opted to get your books produced by an established standard printing company. There are reasons why you might make such a choice. For example, you might require heavier or different paper stock or a high quality binding. There are plenty of such services to choose from and you can often obtain a good quality product for a reasonable price. However, you lose the big advantage of the sales and distribution facilities that come with the link between Amazon and the POD service. Similarly, you won't have the flexibility with order quantities. With POD, you can order as few copies as you wish; a printing company will usually have a minimum order quantity for which you will need to pay up front and store the books. This may be fine if you are planning to sell direct to the public, but not so easy for selling on-line.

Amazon has a facility for people to sell books on-line, however it costs £25 per month if you sell more than 35 books per month otherwise you only pay the 15% commission of the sale price and a closing fee. Amazon takes the order, collects the fees (including postage at typically £2.80) and notifies you of the order. You ship the order and Amazon credit you with the balance. Alternatively you could consider the 'fulfilment by Amazon' option where you send your items to be stored by Amazon who handle the whole sales process. In addition to a monthly storage fee, each sale will be subject to fees for 'pick and pack' and 'weight handling'. Full details can be found at http://services.amazon.co.uk/services.html

E-books

In the world of e-books, Amazon stands alone, offering e-books only for its own e-reader family - the Kindle. While the Kindle continues to enjoy enormous popularity, other devices are gaining prominence and it is worth considering the various options. We discuss e-readers and e-books more generally elsewhere in this book but, in this chapter, we focus on the facilities offered by Amazon. It is estimated [19] that Amazon accounts for 90% of e-book sales in Great Britain.

There are different ways to get your e-book sold through Amazon. Ultimately, it will need to be in an acceptable format for Amazon as they do not use the standard e-pub format - Amazon has their own azw format, but you can submit a mobi file created by KindleGen. Having said that, there is no need for the author to create books in this format; there are many solutions available for which a high level of technical expertise is not required. Most text-only books will present few problems. However, books that require pictures, tables and advanced formatting may require some specialist intervention. We discuss technical issues later in this chapter and elsewhere in this book, but let us first consider the general issue of publishing an e-book on Amazon.

Kindle Direct Publishing (KDP)

KDP is a service offered by Amazon to authors and publishers for the creation and sales of e-books for the Kindle e-reader. Books can be uploaded in a variety of formats and Amazon will perform any required conversion and formatting. Protection against unauthorised copying can be applied by opting for Digital Rights Management (DRM). KDP is free but limits are set on prices and authors can receive up to 70% of the net sales. As this is essentially a US based enterprise, some conditions apply to authors from other countries and an amazon.com account is required to use the service.

The author sets the cover price within limits set by Amazon and should be at least 20% cheaper than any printed version of the book. Amazon also reserves the right to sell at a lower or higher price under certain circumstances. Royalties from e-books sold in the US are liable for tax deductions. Royalties are calculated after delivery costs based upon the file size; currently 10p per megabyte in the UK.

An ISBN is not required as Amazon will assign its own identification and, as the Kindle version is unique to Amazon, there is no real advantage in supplying one. However, if the author has an ISBN that they really wish to use, then this can be submitted, but this must be unique to the Kindle e-book. If the e-book is offered to other retailers in another format such as epub, then a separate ISBN will be required.

To sign up for KDP, the user will require an amazon.com account, so UK authors will usually need to set up a separate account from the one that they have with amazon.co.uk. When setting up your Kindle publishing details you will probably want to add your bank details so that you can be paid by electronic transfer when your royalties reach a minimum of £10 in any sales domain. There is a button to click for adding a bank account and you can then enter the required details. Note that you will need to supply an IBAN (International Bank Account Number) and a BIC (Branch Identifier Code). These are different from the account number and sort code that you normally use and you can get them from your printed bank statement.

Before you submit your book to KDP it is worth doing a little preparation. If you are using Word and intend to submit the book in this format, ensure that it contains minimal formatting and no page numbers. However, if you want to be sure that everything will be all right, then use the Kindlegen software to produce a e-book version that you can inspect. If your book contains images or tables, then this is really worthwhile.

The process of publishing an e-book for Kindle is basically very simple. Having set up an account, the e-book can be uploaded together with some accompanying information including a cover image for marketing. Amazon state that the e-book will normally be available for sale online within 12 hours. Before you start the process, take the time to read the 'Getting Started' guide at:

https://kdp.amazon.com/help?topicId=A37Z49E2DDQPP3

The author retains the copyright and can withdraw the book at any time. Also, there are no restrictions on publishing elsewhere, although this will require conversion to another format and separate retail agreements.

Amazon provide an option called KDP Select that offers a free download service for Amazon Prime customers via the Kindle Owners' Lending Library and the author gets paid a fixed sum for each download. This may seem an attractive option but might not be advisable because Amazon demands exclusive sales rights for this service over a 90 day period. Authors should carefully consider the merits and demerits of any distributor or retailer that demands exclusivity.

For Kindle book sales, Amazon offers a choice of two different royalty options: 70% or 35%. The 70% option incurs a 'delivery fee' in the region of 10p per megabyte, but generally it will be better to select this option. The 70% applies to the retail price (which may be lower than the list price set by the author) and is available on sales only in Amazon's 'available sales territories'. Also with this option, the list price must be at least 20% lower than any printed edition of the same work and it must be between £1.49 and £7.81 (prices at 4th June 2014).

The 35% option is less restrictive and has a maximum list price of £120. The minimum list price depends upon the file size and varies from £0.75 for a file size up to 3 megabytes to £1.49 for files larger than 10 megabytes.

For either royalty option, the reader is advised to check the conditions, requirements and latest prices on Amazon's website. See also chapter 6 for further information on pricing and details of VAT on e-books.

Your Kindle book will normally need two covers: one to display on the Kindle and the other to display on Amazon (the product image). These do not have to be the same, although some similarity is useful to avoid any confusion. The cover image that gets displayed on the Kindle should be 1563 x 2500 pixels for best quality or a minimum of 625 x 1000. Amazon also recommends that the image should be in RGB colour mode because although the standard Kindles are monochrome, there are now colour versions and also other devices can read Kindle books with a suitable app. They also recommend using a narrow border if the image has a white background. The image should be uploaded in JPEG or TIFF format.

The product image needs to be an eye-catching picture to attract people to buy your book. Amazon's general rules for product images state a minimum image size of 1280 x 2560 pixels, be in JPEG or TIFF format and follow their convention for naming. Thus, a typical filename would use the ISBN-13 code without any dashes or spaces with an option 4 character variant code, for example 9781908837004.MAIN.JPG or just 9781908837004.JPG for a book with ISBN 978-1-908837-00-4. Amazon suggests that RGB images for display on a computer monitor should use the working colour format sRGB. This can be done with suitable image editing software e.g. PhotoShop, if available.

So now that you have your e-book on sale with Amazon; how are you going to sell lots of copies? For one thing, you are just one among many authors who have done exactly the same thing. If your book is non-fiction, then there's a chance that potential customers will come across your book whilst browsing for a particular topic. If your book is fiction then you are in a big pool and your book must strongly identify with a particular genre e.g. horror, romantic, science fiction etc. Another thing is that it is trickier to have the 'sell direct' equivalent of physical books so this avenue is probably not worth considering. You may have to rely on support from Amazon for the promotion of your e-book, even if this means offering it at a very low price for a limited period. Some e-book writers attribute their success to a short-term free offer but as so many people are doing this now, you might still go unnoticed and miss out on a few sales. In 2012 Waterstones surprised many people by doing a deal with Amazon in which they agreed to sell the Kindle and Amazon e-books in its stores, so you could see your e-book on sale in the high street. You can now 'Read for Free' in a Waterstones store with your Kindle. Customers can download eligible books in a UK Waterstones store and read them for free for one hour each day.

You don't have to go through KDP in order to get your e-book listed on Amazon, so what are the alternatives and how do they compare? We can forget CreateSpace for a start because that is an Amazon company and you just get directed to KDP.

Blurb can create e-books but, at the time of writing, only sell through their own shop-front or the Apple iBookstore. Lulu offer e-book sales to a variety of channels, including Amazon. SmashWords don't currently include an option for distribution on Amazon. Other companies provide e-book services e.g. Autharium offers a free e-book publishing service and sells through Amazon, Barnes & Noble, Waterstones, iBooks, Kobo, W.H. Smith, Foyles etc. It offers 85% of net returns to the author and supplies some resources to the author.

Concluding Remarks

Amazon is a very useful resource for self publishing authors and could probably be considered essential for physical books. With regard to e-books, there are viable alternatives and it may be worth distributing across different platforms even if this means creating two formats and obtaining separate ISBNs.

A common complaint about self published books, and e-books in particular, is the poor standard of spelling and grammar used. Readers get annoyed with books that are riddled with spelling and grammatical errors and are likely to write bad reviews resulting in lost sales. The use of spell and grammar checkers should be routine these days and, while they won't pick up all errors, they can be an enormous help. It is still recommended that all books have some form of proofreading by a suitable person.

Finally, if you are creating an e-book, make sure it is properly formatted for Kindle or other e-readers. This is best done by preparing the necessary files yourself and loading them onto your own reader or an emulator.

GLOSSARY OF TERMS

AZW: A file format used by Amazon for Kindle books.

Binding: The cover of a book holding the pages together.

Bleed: Printing that goes to the edge of the sheet after trimming.

Bulk: Thickness of paper stock in thousandths of an inch or number of pages per inch.

Case bind: A type of binding used in making hard cover books using glue.

Comb bind: To plastic comb bind by inserting the comb into punched holes.

Cover paper: A heavy printing paper used to cover books, make presentation folders, etc.

Crop marks: Printed lines showing where to trim a printed sheet.

Crossover: Printing across the gutter or from one page to the facing page of a publication.

Density: The degree of colour or darkness of an image or photograph.

DRM: Digital Rights Management - a system used to protect e-books from being copied.

E-book: An electronic book that can be read on a computer or dedicated reading device.

Epub: A file format used by a variety of e-readers.

E-Reader: A small, portable device for reading e-books.

Flood: To cover a printed page with ink, varnish, or plastic coating.

Flop: The reverse side of an image.

Foil stamping: Using a die to place a metallic or pigmented image on paper.

Galley proof: Text copy before it is put into a mechanical layout or desktop layout.

Gutter: The inside margin of a page within a book.

Halftone: Converting a continuous tone to dots for printing.

HTML: HyperText Markup Language - used for web pages and e-books.

ISBN: International Standard Book Number. A 10 or 13 digit number that uniquely identifies a book.

JPEG: A format for storing images in a compressed form.

Laminate: To cover with film, to bond or glue one surface to another.

Lines per inch: The number of rows of dots per inch in a halftone.

Matte finish: Dull paper or ink finish.

Mobi: File format used by Amazon and produced from the KindleGen software.

Offset Lithography: A printing method using a plate and inked rollers.

Opacity: The amount of show-through on a printed sheet.

PCX: A format for storing compressed image files without loss of detail.

PDF: Portable Document Format - a popular file format for storing and displaying documents.

Perfect bind: A type of binding that glues the edge of sheets to a cover.

Point: For paper, a unit of thickness 1/1000 inch. for typesetting, a unit of height 1/72 inch.

PostScript: The computer language most recognized by printing devices.

POD: Print on Demand - an automated form of book production for short runs.

Recto: The right-hand page of an open book.

Resolution / Definition: Refers to the number of dots per inch in a digital image. A higher dpi will be better quality.

Saddle stitch: Binding a booklet or magazine with staples in the seam where it folds.

Sans serif: Typefaces that do not feature serifs.

Serif: Small lines in the characters of certain typefaces.

Side stitch: Binding by stapling along one side of a sheet.

Spine: The binding edge of a book or publication.

Stamping: Term for foil stamping.

Stock: The material to be printed.

TIFF: Tagged Image File Format. Widely used in publishing.

Trim marks: Similar to crop or register marks. They show where to trim the printed sheet.

Trim size: The final size of one printed image after the last trim is made.

Verso: The left-hand page of an open book.

Vignette halftone: A halftone whose background gradually fades to white.

BIBLIOGRAPHY

[1]   Amazon Kindle Publishing Guidelines, v 2014.1.1,
        Amazon Web Services

[2]   Humphreys, J. "Lost for Words", 2004, Hodder,
        ISBN 0-340-83659-8

[3]   Rich, J. "Self Publishing for Dummies", 2006 Wiley,
        ISBN 0-471-79952-1

[4]   Rosenthal, M. "Print-On-Demand Book Publishing",
        2008, Foner Books, ISBN 0-9723801-3-2

[5]   Shepard, A. "POD for Profit", 2010, Shepard
        Publications, ISBN 978-0-938497-46-2

[6]   Shepard, A. "Aiming at Amazon", 2009 Shepard
        Publications, ISBN 978-0-938497-43-1

[7]   Wodehouse, P.G. "Sunset at Blandings",1977, Penguin,
        ISBN 0-14-012448-9

[8]   http://www.britannica.com/EBchecked/topic/
        482597/history-of-publishing#toc28596

[9]   http://www.isbn.org/standards/home/isbn/us/
        Isbnqa.asp#Q9

[10]   http://www.isbn.nielsenbook.co.uk/, Nielsen UK ISBN
        Agency

[11]   http://bookcovers.creativindie.com/free-online-isbn-
        barcode-generator/

[12]   http://www.writersworld.co.uk

[13] http://www.ondemandbooks.com

[14] http://www.lightningsource.com/
      GlobalDistChannels.aspx

[15] http://www.sylviamilne.co.uk/libcats.htm

[16] http://www.gutenberg.org/, "Free ebooks", 2014

[17] http://www.oxforddictionaries.com/definition/
      english/self-publish

[18] http://www.zeuspublications.com/
      subsidy_publishing.htm, "Subsidy or
      PartnershipPublishing", 2014

[19] http://www.guardian.co.uk/technology/2012/
      oct/24/amazon-tax-loophole-ebooks

[20] http://www.thebookseller.com/news/
      January-2015-tax-change-e-book-downloads.html

[21] http://www.copyright.gov/circs/circ15a.pdf,
      "Duration of Copyright", 2011

INDEX

www.ingramcontent.com/pod-product-compliance
Lightning Source LLC
Chambersburg PA
CBHW061447040426
42450CB00007B/1258